SKILLS MASTERY & TEST PRACTICE

This Book Includes:

- **Access to Online SBAC Practice Assessments**
  - Two Performance Tasks (PT)
  - Two Computer Adaptive Tests (CAT)
  - Self-paced learning and personalized score reports
  - Strategies for building speed and accuracy
  - Instant feedback after completion of the Assessments
- **Standards based practice**
  - Reading: Literature
  - Reading: Informational Text
  - Language
- **Detailed answer explanations for every question**

Complement Classroom Learning All Year

Using the Lumos Study Program, parents and teachers can reinforce the classroom learning experience for children. It creates a collaborative learning platform for students, teachers and parents.

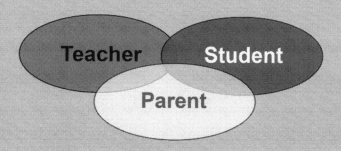

Used in Schools
To Improve Student Achievement

Lumos Learning

SBAC Test Prep: Grade 4 English Language Arts Literacy (ELA) Common Core Practice Book and Full-length Online Assessments: Smarter Balanced Study Guide

Contributing Author   -   Mary Evans Rumley
Contributing Editor   -   Julie Turner
Curriculum Director   -   Marisa Adams
Executive Producer   -   Mukunda Krishnaswamy
Designer and Illustrator - Harini N.

ISBN-10: 1940484766

ISBN-13: 978-1-940484-76-1

Printed in the United States of America

For permissions and additional information contact us

Lumos Information Services, LLC
PO Box 1575, Piscataway, NJ 08855-1575
http://www.LumosLearning.com

Email: support@lumoslearning.com
Tel: (732) 384-0146
Fax: (866) 283-6471

Lumos Learning

Table of Contents

Introduction

The Common Core State Standards Initiative (CCSS) was created from the need to have more robust and rigorous guidelines which could be standardized from state to state. These guidelines create a learning environment where students will be able to graduate high school with all skills necessary to be active and successful members of society, whether they take a role in the workforce or in some sort of post-secondary education.

Once the CCSS were fully developed and implemented, it became necessary to devise a way to ensure they were assessed appropriately. To this end, states adopting the CCSS have joined one of two consortia, either PARCC or Smarter Balanced.

What is SBAC?

The Smarter Balanced Assessment Consortium (SBAC) is one of the two state consortiums responsible for developing assessments aligned to the rigorous Common Core State Standards. Thousands of educators, along with test developers, have worked together to create the new computer based English Language Arts and Math Assessments.

SBAC's first round of testing occurred during the 2014 – 2015 school year. The tests are conducted online, requiring students complete tasks to assess a deeper understanding of the CCSS and will involve a variety of new technology-enhanced question.

How Can the Lumos Study Program Prepare Students for SBAC Tests?

At Lumos Learning, we believe that year-long learning and adequate practice before the actual test are the keys to success on these standardized tests. We have designed the Lumos study program to help students get plenty of realistic practice before the test and to promote year-long collaborative learning.

This is a Lumos tedBook™. It connects you to Online SBAC Assessments and additional resources using a number of devices including Android phones, iPhones, tablets and personal computers. The Lumos StepUp Online Assessment is designed to promote year-long learning. It is a simple program students can securely access using a computer or device with internet access. Students will get instant feedback and can review their answers anytime. Each student's answers and progress can be reviewed by parents and educators to reinforce the learning experience.

How to access the Lumos SBAC Online Assessments

First Time Access:

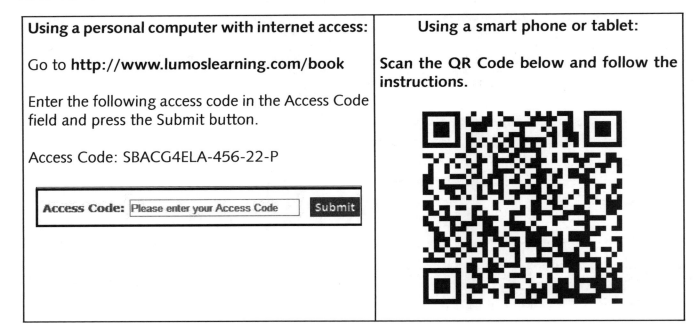

Using a personal computer with internet access:	Using a smart phone or tablet:
Go to **http://www.lumoslearning.com/book**	Scan the QR Code below and follow the instructions.
Enter the following access code in the Access Code field and press the Submit button.	
Access Code: SBACG4ELA-456-22-P	

In the next screen, click on the "New User" button to register your user name and password.

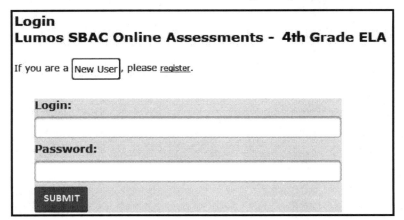

Login
Lumos SBAC Online Assessments - 4th Grade ELA

If you are a New User, please register.

Login:

Password:

SUBMIT

Subsequent Access:

After you establish your user id and password for subsequent access, simply login with your account information.

What if I buy more than one Lumos Study Program?

Please note that you can use all Online SBAC Assessments with one User ID and Password. If you buy more than one book, you will access them with the same account.

Go back to the **http://www.lumoslearning.com/book** link and enter the access code provided in the second book. In the next screen simply login using your previously created account.

How to create a teacher account

- You can use the Lumos online programs along with this book to complement and extend your classroom instruction.

- Get a Free Teacher account by visiting LumosLearning.com/a/sbacbasic

  This Lumos StepUp® Basic teacher account will help you:

  - Create up to 30 student accounts.
  - Review the online work of your students.
  - Easily access CCSS.
  - Create and share information about your classroom or school events.
  - Recommend useful mobile apps and books to your students.

  NOTE: There is a limit of one grade and subject per teacher for the free account.

- Download the Lumos SchoolUp™ mobile app using the instructions provided in "How can I Download the App?" section of this chapter.

- To learn more about the teacher portal please refer to "Lumos StepUp® Teacher Portal FAQ" section of this book.

QR code for Teacher account

Test Taking Tips

1) **The day before the test,** make sure you get a good night's sleep.

2) **On the day of the test,** be sure to eat a good hearty breakfast! Also, be sure to arrive at school on time.

3) **During the test:**

- **Read every question carefully.**

  - Do not spend too much time on any one question. Work steadily through all questions in the section.
  - Attempt all of the questions even if you are not sure of some answers.
  - If you run into a difficult question, eliminate as many choices as you can and then pick the best one from the remaining choices. Intelligent guessing will help you increase your score.
  - Also, mark the question so that if you have extra time, you can return to it after you reach the end of the section.
  - Some questions may refer to a graph, chart, or other kind of picture. Carefully review the graphic before answering the question.
  - Be sure to include explanations for your written responses and show all work.

- **While Answering Multiple-Choice (EBSR) questions.**

  - Select the bubble corresponding to your answer choice.
  - Read **all** of the answer choices, even if think you have found the correct answer.

- **While Answering TECR questions.**

  - Read the directions of each question. Some might ask you to drag something, others to select, and still others to highlight. Follow all instructions of the question (or questions if it is in multiple parts)

How to use this book effectively

The Lumos Program is a flexible learning tool. It can be adapted to suit a student's skill level and the time available to practice before standardized tests. Here are some tips to help you use this book and the online resources effectively:

Students

- The standards in each book can be practiced in the order designed, or in the order of your own choosing.
- Complete all problems in each workbook.
- Take the first practice CAT and PT online.
- Download the Lumos StepUp® app using the instructions provided in "How can I Download the App?" to have anywhere access to online resources.
- Have open-ended questions evaluated by a teacher or parent, keeping in mind the scoring rubrics.
- Take the second CAT and PT as you get close to the official test date.
- Complete the test in a quiet place, following the test guidelines. Practice tests provide you an opportunity to improve your test taking skills and to review topics included in the CCSS related standardized test.

Parents

- Familiarize yourself with the SBAC test format and expectations.
- Get useful information about your school by downloading the Lumos SchoolUp™ app. Please follow directions provided in "How can I Download the App?" section of this chapter.
- Help your child use Lumos StepUp® SBAC Online Assessments by following the instructions in "How to access the Lumos SBAC Online Assessments" section of this chapter.
- Review your child's performance in the "Lumos SBAC Online Assessments" periodically. You can do this by simply asking your child to log into the system online and selecting the subject area you wish to review.

Reading: Literature

Finding Detail in the Story (RL.4.1)

"The Elephant Who Saw the World . . .," Mary started speaking. It was Friday, and the students had to share their creative writing stories of the week.

Mary loved writing, and this was her favorite part of the week, when they were able to make up stories for creative writing. She enjoyed it so much that she became really good at it. Even at home on the weekends when she didn't have much homework, she would sit in her room for hours and create stories to share with her friends and family. Her parents always supported her and were her biggest fans.

However, there was one part about every Friday at school that Mary did not enjoy, and that was when she had to share her story in front of the class. The teacher made all of the children share on Friday afternoons, and this made Mary very nervous. She was shy, and although she knew her teacher was right, she didn't like it.

Sitting and listening to the other children, Mary heard her name called. It was her turn to share. She got out of her seat slowly, walked to the front of the room and began.

Question Number: 1

What is the title of Mary's story?

Ⓐ **The Elephant Who Liked Candy**
Ⓑ **The Elephant Who Saw the World**
Ⓒ **The Elephant Who Wanted to See the World**
Ⓓ **The Girl who Hated Writing**

Question Number: 2

What didn't Mary like doing?

Ⓐ **Writing stories**
Ⓑ **Having her stories corrected by the teacher**
Ⓒ **Reading her stories in front of the class**
Ⓓ **Going to school**

Question Number: 3

Why was Mary reading her story in front of the class?

Ⓐ **It was something she loved to do.**
Ⓑ **Her classmates asked her to.**
Ⓒ **Every Friday the children had to share their creative writing stories.**
Ⓓ **Her parents wanted her to.**

Ellie the Ostrich has had a very difficult time lately. Her friends Bailey and Jose run and play with her, but when they play tag she always loses! They start running and before she knows it, Bailey and Jose are fluttering around her head. And they are such small birds! She is the largest bird in the world, but she cannot fly. No matter how hard she flaps her wings, they just won't lift her off the ground. Her legs are so strong and long that she can travel faster by running. But Ellie doesn't want to run, she wants to fly and fly.

One day, her father notices how sad she is as her friends fly away. He calls her to sit under the tree. "I know how hard it is to watch your smaller friends fly away, my sweet Ellie. But do you know how special your wings are?"

"No, Daddy." Ellie's feather fly as she shakes her head back and forth.

"You can use your wings to help gather speed when you start to run. You can also use them as brakes when turning and stopping which lets you stop very fast! In fact, our ostrich cousins have been known to run at a rate of 60 miles an hour which is faster than horses can run and as fast as most people drive cars."

"I can outrun a car?" she asks incredulously.

Ellie's dad grins. "You certainly can!"

"Wow. I think the next time they suggest tag, I'm going to suggest a race instead!"

Question Number: 4

What is a detail that supports why Ellie travels faster by running?

Ⓐ **Her legs are so strong and long that she can travel faster by running.**
Ⓑ **She can also use them as brakes in turning and stopping.**
Ⓒ **No matter how hard she flaps her wings, they just won't lift her off the ground.**
Ⓓ **Ellie doesn't want to run, she wants to fly and fly.**

Question Number: 5

According to Ellie's father, how do ostriches use their wings?

Ⓐ **to help them to fly**
Ⓑ **as brakes while running**
Ⓒ **by flapping them**
Ⓓ **to keep them warm**

Alex the Great

Nearly two thousand five hundred years ago, there lived a king called Alexander the Great. He was the son of Philip II of Macedonia. When Alexander was a boy, a magnificent horse for sale was brought to the court of his father. The animal was to be sold for thirteen talents. Talents are ancient coins. Many were eager to buy the horse, but none could get close enough to saddle the restless animal. He was wild, and it was impossible to ride him.

Alexander pleaded with his father to let him try. Realizing that the horse was terrified of its own shadow, he turned the horse towards the sun so that its shadow fell behind it. This calmed the horse, and the prince proudly rode away. Observing this, his father said, "My son, look for a kingdom worthy of your greatness. Macedonia is too small for you."

That is exactly what Alexander tried to do when he grew up. He fought many battles and always rode Bucephalus (that was the horse's name.) Friendship and trust grew between man and horse. When Bucephalus died of wounds received in battle, Alexander was heartbroken and deeply mourned the loss of his horse. He wished that he had died along with it.

Question Number: 6

How did Alexander calm the horse when he was for sale?

Ⓐ **He saddled and rode him.**
Ⓑ **He talked in a soothing voice.**
Ⓒ **He pleaded with his father to let him try.**
Ⓓ **He turned the horse so he couldn't see his shadow.**

One day, Ellie the Ostrich watched as two men entered her Aunt and Uncle's house. Moments later, they came out with a handful of eggs. "Mama! Mama!" Ellie cried, running into her own house.

"What is it sweet?"

"The eggs, Mama! They're stealing the eggs!" Tugging her mother's wings she pulled her out of the house and into the yard, watching with sad eyes as the men placed the eggs in special crates and drove off.

"Oh, honey, they're not stealing them." Ellie's mama explained. "These are eggs that will not become babies. Ostrich eggs are very special and the humans love to use them for food. They also make jewlery and cups with the egg shells."

Ellie's eyes got wider and wider as her mother continued talking. "Wow. They like our eggs that much and they weren't stealing them?"

"They do, Ellie and no, your Aunt and Uncle knew they were coming today. But, you did a wonderful job letting us know." "I did?"

Spreading a large wing, Ellie's mother pulled her in for a hug. "Of course you did. Protecting our family is one of the most important jobs we will ever have and you did that beautifully!"

Question Number: 7

Which detail describes the way ostrich eggs are used?

Ⓐ **Ostriches have been known to run at the rate of 60 miles an hour.**
Ⓑ **Each Ostrich egg weighs one pound, which is as much as two dozen chicken eggs.**
Ⓒ **The shells also are made into cups and ornaments.**
Ⓓ **Ostrich eggs are delicious.**

This year Jim and I had the most wonderful vacation compared to the one we took last year. We went to Hawaii, which is a much better place to visit than a hunting lodge in Alaska. The hotel we stayed in was a luxury suite. It included a big screen TV with all of the movie channels, a hot tub on the balcony, a small kitchen stocked with local fruits and vegetables, and a huge bed shaped like a pineapple. The weather in Hawaii could not have been any better. We enjoyed many hours on the beach sunbathing and playing volleyball. When we were not on the beach, we were in the ocean swimming or riding the waves on a surf board. Each night we enjoyed eating and dancing with all of our friends at a luau. Our week in Hawaii rushed by, making us wish we had planned a two-week vacation.

Conversely, the hunting lodge in Alaska that we stayed in had no TV, a shower with barely warm water, a small cooler for our food, and cots to sleep on each night. Furthermore, the room wasn't even the worst part of the vacation. The weather was terrible. It rained the entire time we were there. Even with the rain, our guide expected us to go on the all-day fishing trip that was part of our vacation package. All we caught on that fishing trip was a cold from the rain. After the third day in Alaska, we decided to end our nightmare, cut our trip short, and head for home. Without a doubt, we will be going back to Hawaii next year on our vacation.

Question Number: 8

Which statement supports the author's opinion that their Alaska vacation was miserable?

Ⓐ **Our week in Hawaii rushed by, making us wish we had planned a two-week vacation.**
Ⓑ **The weather in Hawaii could not have been better.**
Ⓒ **This year Jim and I had the most wonderful vacation compared to the one we took last year in Alaska.**
Ⓓ **After the third day in Alaska, we decided to end our nightmare, cut our trip short, and head for home.**

Question Number: 9

Which statement supports the author's opinion that their Hawaii vacation was wonderful?

(A) Our week in Hawaii rushed by, making us wish we had planned a two-week vacation.

(B) The weather in Hawaii could not have been better.

(C) This year Jim and I had the most wonderful vacation compared to the one we took last year in Alaska.

(D) After the third day in Alaska, we decided to end our nightmare, cut our trip short, and head for home.

Question Number: 10

Which detail describes where they stayed in their favorite vacation?

(A) The hunting lodge that we stayed in had no TV, a shower with barely warm water, a small cooler for our food, and cots to sleep on each night.

(B) It included a big screen TV with all of the movie channels, a hot tub on the balcony, a small kitchen stocked with local fruits and vegetables, and a huge bed shaped like a pineapple.

(C) The weather in Hawaii could not have been any better. We enjoyed many hours on the beach sunbathing and playing volleyball.

(D) When we were not on the beach, we were in the ocean swimming or riding the waves on a surf board. Each night we enjoyed eating and dancing with all of our friends at a luau.

Inferring (RL.4.1)

I found a shell, a curly one;
Lying on the sand.
I picked it up and took it home,
Held tightly in my hand.
Mommy looked at it and then,
She held it to my ear,
And from the shell there came a song
Soft and sweet and clear.
I was surprised, I listened hard,
And it was really true:
If you can find a nice big shell,
You'll hear the singing too.
--Unknown

Question Number: 1

Why was the poet surprised?

Ⓐ **She found a shell.**
Ⓑ **Her mother put it to her ear.**
Ⓒ **She didn't expect to hear a song from the shell.**
Ⓓ **She was frightened of the shell.**

Alex the Great

Nearly two thousand five hundred years ago, there lived a king called Alexander the Great. He was the son of Philip II of Macedonia. When Alexander was a boy, a magnificent horse was brought to the court of his father, for sale. The animal was to be sold for thirteen talents. Talents are ancient coins. Many were eager to buy the horse, but none could get close enough to saddle the restless animal. He was wild, and it was not possible to ride him.

Alexander pleaded with his father to let him try. Realizing that the horse was terrified of its own shadow, he turned the horse towards the sun so that its shadow fell behind it. This calmed the horse, and the prince proudly rode away. Observing this, his father said, "My son, look for a kingdom worthy of your greatness. Macedonia is too small for you." And that is exactly what Alexander tried to do when he grew up. He fought many battles and always rode Bucephalus. That was the horse's name. Friendship and trust grew between man and horse. When Bucephalus died of wounds received in battle, Alexander was heartbroken and deeply mourned the loss of his horse. He wished that he had died along with it.

Question Number: 2

According to the passage, why do you think the horse was unrideable and wild?

Ⓐ **Because it was angry**
Ⓑ **Because it was hungry**
Ⓒ **Because it was scared**
Ⓓ **Because it was good at riding**

Cindy's mom called her to supper. Cindy looked at the food on the stove and made a face. She went and looked inside the freezer. She saw a frozen pizza and asked her mom if she could cook it.

Question Number: 3

What can you infer from Cindy's actions?

Ⓐ **That she was excited about what her mother had cooked**
Ⓑ **That she was not hungry**
Ⓒ **That she didn't think the meal was ready**
Ⓓ **That she didn't like what her mother had cooked**

Mary loved writing, and this was her favorite part of the week, when they were able to make up stories for creative writing. She enjoyed it so much that she became really good at it. Even at home on the weekends when she didn't have much homework, she would sit in her room for hours and create stories to share with her friends and family. Her parents always supported her and were her biggest fans.

However, there was one part about every Friday at school that Mary did not enjoy, and that was when she had to share her story in front of the class. The teacher made all of the children share on Friday afternoons, and this made Mary very nervous. She was shy, and although she knew her teacher was right, she didn't like it.

Sitting and listening to the other children, Mary heard her name called. It was her turn to share. She got out of her seat slowly, walked to the front of the room and began.

Question Number: 4

What do you think Mary did next?

Ⓐ **Began running out of the classroom because she was scared**
Ⓑ **Began reading her story in front of the class**
Ⓒ **Began to cry**
Ⓓ **Began to tell the teacher that she really couldn't read her story**

Question Number: 5

Why did Mary's parents support her love for writing stories?

Ⓐ So that she wouldn't sit in front of the tv all day
Ⓑ To keep her busy
Ⓒ Because she liked to write and was good at it
Ⓓ None of the above

As Ben woke up on Sunday, he was thinking that it would be great to do something special with his dad that day, as he didn't see him very often. When he looked outside the window, he noticed that the sun was out but a new blanket of snow had fallen during the night. He was getting dressed thinking of what they could do when all of a sudden he heard his dad say, "It is a sunny day. Grab your skiis on the way down!" Ben ran to get his skiis and they left.

Question Number: 6

Where do you think Ben and his dad were going?

Ⓐ to the zoo
Ⓑ to the mall
Ⓒ to the local mountain
Ⓓ to school

Thelma lay on the windowsill. She heard a loud noise, so she lifted her head and looked outside. It woke her up and now she wasn't happy. The color of the sky was changing from dark to a light pinkish yellow. She could hear the birds starting to chirp. She figured it was time to go and find some food as she was starting to get hungry.

Question Number: 7

What time of day do you think this is happening?

Ⓐ in the evening at sunset
Ⓑ in the early afternoon
Ⓒ in the early morning at sunrise
Ⓓ none of the above

Question Number: 8

What kind of animal is Thelma?

Ⓐ a horse
Ⓑ a cricket
Ⓒ a mouse
Ⓓ a cat

Before going to bed on Friday night, Susie's parents told her they had a surprise planned for the weekend and she would have to wake up really early on Saturday morning. When she woke up, they left the house quickly and started driving. While in the car, Susie looked outside to see if she could figure out where they were going. She noticed that it was getting really hot out and the sun was shining brightly. Then she noticed that the surfboards were in the car. Finally, they stopped, and Susie said, "I know where we are going!"

Question Number: 9

What season is it?

Ⓐ **Summer**
Ⓑ **Spring**
Ⓒ **Winter**
Ⓓ **Fall**

Question Number: 10

Where do Susie and her family probably live?

Ⓐ **in Alaska**
Ⓑ **close to the beach**
Ⓒ **in the mountains**
Ⓓ **in Arkansas**

Finding the Theme (RL.4.2)

Fred....dentist

Fred had never been to the dentist. All of his life he had heard horror stories about the buzzing drills, the huge needles, and the scary tools that the dentist used to torture his patients. Since none of his teeth were hurting, Fred just couldn't understand why his mom was insisting on taking him to see one. She told him that it was important to visit the dentist each year to have your teeth checked and to get your teeth cleaned. That was just silly to Fred since he cleaned his teeth everyday by brushing and flossing them, but nothing would change his mother's mind. He found it hard to believe that she would think it was a good idea to take him somewhere to be tortured. However, he had no choice but to go.

On the way to the dentist, Fred's imagination went wild. He pictured walking into a room with a huge chair that the dentist would strap him to. He could just see the dentist pulling out a huge drill and drilling his tooth while his mother and several others held him in the chair. By the time he got to the dentist's office, he was shaking all over.

To his surprise, the office was nothing like he expected. The dentist was nice, and the chair was comfortable and didn't have any straps with which to tie him to it. He looked around the room and didn't see any huge drills or torture devices. He was relieved when all the dentist did was look in his mouth, show him how to properly brush and floss his teeth, and give him a balloon. His mom made an appointment to have his teeth cleaned. Maybe this wouldn't be as bad as he had thought it would be.

Question Number: 1

What is the theme of the above passage?

Ⓐ **Dentists are good people.**
Ⓑ **Moms know best.**
Ⓒ **Things are usually not as bad as you think they will be.**
Ⓓ **Imagination is good.**

Opal walked into the store not wanting to do what she had planned. She knew when she took the makeup without paying for it that it was wrong. She felt so guilty. She knew she couldn't keep the makeup. So, gathering all of her courage, she walked up to the security officer and confessed what she had done. He admonished her for shoplifting but let her off with a warning because she had been honest. She felt very relieved.

Question Number: 2

What is the theme of the above passage?

Ⓐ **The unknown can be scary.**
Ⓑ **It is best to be honest.**
Ⓒ **Don't cry over spilled milk.**
Ⓓ **Mom knows best.**

Libby's grandmother didn't have much money, so she couldn't buy Libby an expensive present for Christmas like her other grandmother could. She didn't want to buy her some cheap toy that wouldn't last long, but she just couldn't afford the things that were on Libby's wish list. She decided that she would make Libby a quilt. She was afraid her granddaughter wouldn't like the gift, but it was the best that she could do.

When Christmas day arrived, Grandmother went to Libby's house. She saw all of the nice gifts that her granddaughter had received. She was worried as Libby began to open her present. Libby squealed with delight when she saw the handmade quilt. She ran and hugged her grandmother and thanked her. She ran and put the new quilt on her bed. The rest of the day she talked about how much she loved the quilt, especially since her grandmother had made it all by hand.

Question Number: 3

What is the theme of the above passage?

Ⓐ **It is not the cost of the gift that matters but the thought and love put into it.**
Ⓑ **Expensive gifts are better than homemade ones.**
Ⓒ **Homemade gifts are as good as expensive toys.**
Ⓓ **Good manners have positive results.**

Question Number: 4

Which of the following is NOT the theme of this passage?

Ⓐ **It's not the cost of the gift that matters.**
Ⓑ **Expensive gifts are better than homemade ones.**
Ⓒ **A gift from the heart is valuable.**
Ⓓ **A gift made with love is the best gift of all.**

Today was Rhonda's first day at her new school. She wished that she was going back to her old school, but that was impossible since they had moved. Although she didn't have many friends at her old school, she still would prefer it because she knew the teachers and the rules.

The first day, Rhonda met three girls that she really liked. They had all of their classes together. Best of all, this school had art and music class. Her old school had neither. Rhonda and her new friends had a great time in art that first day. She couldn't wait to go to music tomorrow. Maybe this new school wouldn't be so bad after all.

Question Number: 5

What is the theme of the above passage?

Ⓐ **Friends help each other.**
Ⓑ **Bullying hurts everyone.**
Ⓒ **Change can be good.**
Ⓓ **It's OK to be different.**

Polly's little brother begged her to read him a story. She told him to go away, that she didn't have time to bother with him. A few minutes later, he came back and asked her again. This time she yelled at him to go away. She heard him crying as he ran down the hall. Later when she went to the family room, her mother told her that she had hurt her brother's feelings. Polly looked over at him and told him that she was sorry. Although she apologized, her little brother's feelings were still hurt. He felt like Polly didn't like to spend time with him. Polly's mom told her that sometimes words were not enough. So, Polly got his favorite book and asked him to read with her. Her little brother smiled and ran to sit by Polly. He hugged her and told her that she was the best big sister a boy could have.

Question Number: 6

What can you learn from the above passage?

Ⓐ **Knowledge is power.**
Ⓑ **Never give up.**
Ⓒ **Face your fears.**
Ⓓ **Actions speak louder than words.**

Karen and Steve were both in Ms. Taylor's math class. Ms. Taylor wasn't very strict about when they had to turn their work in, and Steve took full advantage of that. He always did his homework for his other classes, but he would put off the work for Ms. Taylor's math assignments thinking he could do them later. However, Karen finished each assignment Ms. Taylor assigned right away. She had to work a little longer each night, but she didn't want to get marked down for turning in her math homework late. At the end of the semester, Karen and Steve both wanted to go to the amusement park. Ms. Taylor called Steve's mother to let her know about Steve not turning the work in on time, and she put Steve on restriction until all of his work was turned in. That was a horrible weekend for Steve. Even though he stayed up really late each night, he still couldn't finish everything. The whole time Steve was working, Karen had a great time eating hot dogs at the amusement park, watching movies, and having a great weekend. When they got their report cards, Steve was lucky to get by with a "C" minus in math while Karen got an "A."

Question Number: 7

What did Karen and Steve learn from this?

Ⓐ **It doesn't matter when you do it as long as it gets done.**
Ⓑ **Lazy people aren't nice.**
Ⓒ **It's better to do things on time instead of putting them off for later.**
Ⓓ **None of the above**

Mr. Toad and Mr. Rabbit were eating at the food court of the shopping mall. Mr. Toad was eating many slices of pizza and drinking a huge soda, and Mr. Rabbit was watching him.

"Hey, Mr. Toad. If you give me some of your pizza, I'll let you have the next fly I find," called out Mr. Rabbit.

Mr. Toad said no, even though he was so full. "I'm sorry, Mr. Rabbit," Mr. Toad said, "but this pizza cost a lot so I can't share it."

Mr. Rabbit was sad and waited for Mr. Toad to finish. They then left the mall together. On their way out the door, a hunter saw them and started running after them. Mr. Toad normally could have escaped, but since he had eaten so much, Mr. Toad couldn't move another inch. The hunter caught him. Mr. Rabbit was able to escape easily.

Question Number: 8

What is the theme of the story?

Ⓐ **It's better to share.**
Ⓑ **If you paid for it, it's all yours.**
Ⓒ **Better late than never**
Ⓓ **None of the above**

Frank studied all the time, and he felt that he was very smart. One day at school, a student from Frank's class asked him if he wanted to go play baseball, but Frank said, "I've read all about baseball in books, and it sounds boring. No, thanks."

Another day, a different student asked Frank if he wanted to go and get hamburgers after school. Frank responded, "I've read that hamburgers are made with beef heart and organ meat. No, thank you."

Nobody wanted to ask Frank to go hang out again, but he did study about why it's important to have friends in his books.

Question Number: 9

What would be an appropriate theme for the above passage?

Ⓐ **It's not nice to be mean to your friends.**
Ⓑ **Friends are always getting in the way.**
Ⓒ **Learning from books is no substitute for real life experience.**
Ⓓ **None of the above**

A monkey put his hand into a jar of cookies. He grasped as many as he could possibly hold, but when he tried to pull out his hand, the neck of the cookie jar prevented him from doing so. Unwilling to lose the cookies, and yet unable to withdraw his hand, he burst into tears and bitterly lamented his disappointment.

Question Number: 10

What would be an appropriate theme for the above passage?

Ⓐ **The grass is always greener on the other side.**
Ⓑ **Always ask before taking.**
Ⓒ **Don't be greedy.**
Ⓓ **Work now and play later.**

Summarizing the Text (RL.4.2)

Mary walked quietly through the house so that she would not wake her parents. Before entering the kitchen, she stood and listened. She wanted to make sure that nobody had heard her and gotten up. She slowly opened the cabinet door, trying to make sure that it didn't squeak. As Mary reached into the cabinet, something warm and furry touched her hand. Mary ran from the kitchen screaming loudly. Her father ran in to see what had happened. He started laughing when he saw their cat Purr Purr sitting quietly in the kitchen cabinet wagging her tail.

Question Number: 1

Choose the best summary of the above text.

Ⓐ **Mary went to the kitchen. She stopped and listened. She opened the cabinet. She screamed. Her dad laughed.**

Ⓑ **Mary snuck quietly into the kitchen. When she opened the cabinet, something touched her hand and made her scream. Her dad came to help and discovered it was their cat in the cabinet.**

Ⓒ **The cat hid in the cabinet and scared Mary when she reached into it.**

Ⓓ **Mary walked into the kitchen after listening to make sure that nobody heard her. She opened the cabinet slowly and felt something touch her. She ran away screaming. She didn't know it was her cat Purr Purr.**

I was so scared when I first learned that I would be having my tooth pulled. I didn't sleep at all the night before the procedure. I was terrified that it would hurt more than I could bear. I was shaking like a leaf when I sat in the dentist chair. He promised me that it would not hurt, but I certainly had my doubts. The dentist then gave me some medicine. When I awoke, my tooth was gone and I didn't remember a thing.

Question Number: 2

Choose the best summary of the above text.

Ⓐ **The writer was scared about having to have a tooth pulled and thought it would hurt. The dentist gave her medicine, and she didn't feel it when her tooth was pulled.**

Ⓑ **The writer was scared. She got her tooth pulled. The dentist gave her medicine.**

Ⓒ **The dentist gave the writer some medicine so that it wouldn't hurt when her tooth was pulled.**

Ⓓ **The writer was scared about having her tooth pulled. She didn't sleep the night be fore. She was terrified. She was shaking like a leaf. The dentist gave her medicine. She didn't feel a thing when he pulled her tooth.**

Huckleberry Hound ran through the yard and into the field next to his house. Suddenly, he put his nose to the ground and started sniffing as he walked. Yep, he definitely smelled a rabbit. He raised his head and howled loudly to let the other dogs know what he had found. Then, he shot after the rabbit like a bolt of lightning. He chased that rabbit for what seemed like hours, but he never caught it. He returned to his yard with his head hanging and his tail tucked between his legs.

Question Number: 3

Choose the best summary of the above text.

Ⓐ **Huckleberry Hound smelled a rabbit. He chased it for a long time, but never caught it.**
Ⓑ **Huckleberry Hound smelled a rabbit. He ran across the yard to the field. He howled so the other dogs would know he found a rabbit. He shot after the rabbit and chased it for a long time. He didn't catch the rabbit. He went home with his head hung down.**
Ⓒ **Huckleberry Hound chased a rabbit.**
Ⓓ **Huckleberry Hound smelled a rabbit. He put his nose to the ground and followed its trail. He definitely smelled a rabbit. He chased it for a long time. He let the other dogs know he had found a rabbit. He didn't catch the rabbit.**

I had been craving chocolate ice cream all day. Finally, school was over and I could go get a huge cone of chocolate ice cream. The line was long, but it was worth the wait. The first taste of my ice cream cone was delicious. Then, the worst thing imaginable happened. I bumped into the person behind me and dropped my ice cream on the floor.

Question Number: 4

Summarize the above text using one sentence.

Ⓐ **I craved ice cream all day, but when I finally got a cone I dropped it on the floor.**
Ⓑ **I craved ice cream all day, but I dropped it.**
Ⓒ **I bought chocolate ice cream, and I bumped into someone and dropped it.**
Ⓓ **The first taste of ice cream was great because I had been craving it all day.**

Opal walked into the store not wanting to do what she had planned. She knew when she took the makeup without paying for it that it was wrong. She felt so guilty. She knew she couldn't keep the makeup. So, gathering all of her courage, she walked up to the security officer and confessed what she had done.

Question Number: 5

Summarize the above text using only one sentence.

Ⓐ **Opal was ashamed of what she did, so she returned it.**
Ⓑ **Opal stole some makeup; however, she returned it because she felt guilty.**
Ⓒ **Opal walked to the store, and she returned the make-up.**
Ⓓ **Open walked to the store and gathered her courage, because she stole some make-up.**

"The Elephant Who Saved the World . . .," Mary started speaking. It was Friday, and they had to share their creative writing stories of the week.

Mary loved writing, and this was her favorite part of the week, when they were able to make up stories for creative writing. She enjoyed it so much that she became really good at it. Even at home on the weekends when she didn't have much homework, she would sit in her room for hours and create stories to share with her friends and family. Her parents always supported her and were her biggest fans.

However, there was one part about every Friday at school that Mary did not enjoy, and that was when she had to share her story in front of the class. The teacher made all of the children share on Friday afternoons, and this made Mary very nervous. She was shy, and although she knew her teacher was right, she didn't like it.

Sitting and listening to the other children, Mary heard her name called. It was her turn to share. She got out of her seat slowly, walked to the front of the room and began.

Question Number: 6

Choose the sentence that best summarizes the paragraph.

Ⓐ **The teacher required each student to read their story out loud.**
Ⓑ **They were presenting creative short stories as part of their Friday share time.**
Ⓒ **Mary loved writing stories, and creative writing was her favorite. She was an excellent writer but hated getting up in front of the class and sharing her work.**
Ⓓ **Mary agreed that it would be good experience, but she still didn't like it.**

Question Number: 7

Which information is NOT necessary for the summary?

Ⓐ **Mary enjoyed creating the stories, but when it came to presenting them, she got really nervous.**
Ⓑ **She enjoyed writing.**
Ⓒ **This was a strong point of hers.**
Ⓓ **None of the above**

Question Number: 8

What would be the best summary for the paragraph above?

Ⓐ Mary wrote a story about an elephant who traveled the world. She loved writing stories and was excited when they had to do one for class. The teacher always asked the students to present their stories to the class during Friday share time. This was the part that Mary didn't like. She got really nervous speaking in front of the class although she knew it would be a good experience. When it was her turn, she took a deep breath and started sharing her story.

Ⓑ Mary wrote a story called "The Elephant Who Saw the World". Her family supported her passion for writing stories because she was so good at it. She was excited when the teacher assigned this for class one day.

Ⓒ "The Elephant Who Saw the World . . .," Mary started speaking. It was Friday, and they had to share their creative writing stories of the week.
Mary loved writing, and this was her favorite part of the week, when they were able to make up stories for creative writing. She enjoyed it so much that she became really good at it. Even at home on the weekends when she didn't have much homework, she would sit in her room for hours and create stories to share with her friends and family. Her parents always supported her and were her biggest fans.
However, there was one part about every Friday at school that Mary did not enjoy, and that was when she had to share her story in front of the class. The teacher made all of the children share on Friday afternoons, and this made Mary very nervous. She was shy, and although she knew her teacher was right, she didn't like it.
Sitting and listening to the other children, Mary heard her name called. It was her turn to share. She got out of her seat slowly, walked to the front of the room and began.

Ⓓ Mary loved writing stories. She wrote one about a donkey traveling the world and had to present it in front of the class. She was nervous about this.

It was a beautiful day outside, and a group of children were playing in the yard of one boy's house. They noticed a bee's nest up on the roof, so they started throwing rocks, sticks, and other items trying to knock it down. The nest moved a little, but it didn't fall to the ground. Instead, hundreds of bees flew out going everywhere.

Robert turned and ran away as fast as he could. "Get down! Get down!" he could hear Louise screaming. Robert dove to the ground as many bees flew over him. He could hear all the other kids doing the same.

The bee's nest was still hanging. John looked around the yard for something really long to use. He noticed his dad's rake sitting by the porch, so he took the rake and ran over to the porch. He swung it as hard as he could, hitting the nest. The nest was dislodged, went flying through the air, and landed near Robert. With a shriek, Robert jumped to his feet and ran to the other side of the yard. The others were also yelping and trying to run away.

Question Number: 9

What is the best summary for the paragraph above?

Ⓐ **None of the below**

Ⓑ **John wanted to destroy a bees' nest with his friends. They destroyed it and had to try and escape when the bees came flying out of it. Everyone was scared.**

Ⓒ **John and his friends were planning to destroy a bees' nest. They started throwing rocks and sticks at the nest. When all the bees started flying out of the nest, the kids started to run trying to escape the bees. The nest was still hanging from the porch so John went and knocked it off using a rake. It landed near Robert who got up really fast and ran to the other side of the yard.**

Ⓓ **John and his friends prepared to destroy a bees' nest. They threw sticks and stones at the nest to knock it off the porch. It didn't work, so John had to do it again. The nest went flying towards Robert who got scared and ran to the other side of the yard.**

Question Number: 10

Which sentence is NOT necessary for the summary?

Ⓐ **He noticed his dad's rake sitting by the porch.**
Ⓑ **The kids wanted to destroy a bees' nest.**
Ⓒ **John and his friends tried to run from the bees that came flying out of their nest when the kids hit it.**
Ⓓ **None of the above**

Describing Characters (RL.4.3)

Timothy

Timothy is a student at my school. He is well-liked by all of the teachers and students. We all know that we can count on Timothy to keep our secrets, to help us if we ask, and to always be on time. We know that he is always honest and expects others to be honest as well.

Last summer, Timothy got a job walking dogs each morning. When school started this year, everyone encouraged him to quit his job, but he decided to keep it. He knew it would be hard to get up every morning at 5 a.m. in order to get all of the dogs walked and then go to school all day. In addition, he planned to sing in the chorus, play basketball, and be a mentor in the tutoring program this year. He knows it will not be easy, but he thinks his hard work will be worth it. He is trying to save enough money to go to a youth camp next summer.

Question Number: 1

According to the above passage, which set of adjectives would you choose to describe Timothy?

- Ⓐ **Responsible and depressed**
- Ⓑ **Trustworthy and thoughtless**
- Ⓒ **Responsible and ambitious**
- Ⓓ **Arrogant and unfriendly**

Question Number: 2

Based on the above passage, what do you think Timothy would do if someone asked him to help them cheat on a test?

- Ⓐ **Help them cheat but ask them not to tell anyone**
- Ⓑ **Tell them that cheating is dishonest and encourage them not to do it**
- Ⓒ **Help them cheat because he doesn't want them to make a bad grade**
- Ⓓ **Tell them to ask someone else to help them cheat.**

Fred....dentist

Fred had never been to the dentist. All of his life he had heard horror stories about the buzzing drills, the huge needles, and the scary tools that the dentist used to torture his patients. Since none of his teeth were hurting, Fred just couldn't understand why his mom was insisting on taking him to see one. She told him that it was important to visit the dentist each year and to get your teeth cleaned. That was just silly to Fred since he cleaned his teeth everyday by brushing and flossing them. But nothing would change his mother's mind. He found it hard to believe that she would think it was a good idea to take him somewhere to be tortured. However, he had no choice but to go.

On the way to the dentist, Fred's imagination went wild. He pictured walking into a room with a huge chair that the dentist would strap him to. He could just see the dentist pulling out a huge drill and drilling his tooth while his mother and several others held him in the chair. By the time he got to the dentist's office, he was shaking all over. To his surprise, the office was nothing like he expected. The dentist was nice and the chair was comfortable and didn't have any straps with which to tie him to it. He looked around the room and didn't see any huge drills or torture devices. All the dentist did was look in his mouth, show him how to properly brush and floss his teeth, and give him a balloon. His mom made an appointment to have his teeth cleaned. Maybe this wouldn't be as bad as he had thought it would be.

Question Number: 3

Based on the above passage, how do you think Fred felt about going to his first visit to the dentist?

Ⓐ **He was excited and looked forward to it.**
Ⓑ **He was afraid and didn't understand why he had to go.**
Ⓒ **He was afraid but wanted to go and see the drills.**
Ⓓ **He was felt shy about meeting the dentist.**

Question Number: 4

How do you think Fred felt after seeing the dentist office and meeting the dentist?

Ⓐ **scared**
Ⓑ **intimidated**
Ⓒ **relieved**
Ⓓ **joyful**

Adam lives with his dad and his older brother Stanley. Adam and Stanley share a room. Most of the time Adam enjoys sharing a room with his brother, but there are times that he wished he had his own room. Being brothers, they have a lot in common; however, they are different in many ways.

Adam likes to spend time with his friends. If he is not with them, he is texting them or playing games with them online. Adam is always busy. He cannot stand to sit around and do nothing. In fact, the only time he is still is when he is sleeping. Adam plays football, basketball, soccer, and baseball. He loves to be involved in whatever is going on at school or at the town's youth center. He spends a lot of his time encouraging people to recycle and even volunteers at the youth center. Although he loves spending time with his friends, he is willing to give up time with them to help others.

Stanley, on the other hand, loves to stay at home. He enjoys activities that can be done alone such as reading, drawing, and spending time with his dogs. Most days after school you can find him at home enjoying one of his favorite activities. He also thinks recycling is important and makes sure his family does it. Although he likes being alone, he enjoys volunteering at the youth center with his brother. He thinks it is important to make a difference in the lives of others, which is why he thinks he would like to be a doctor. Adam and Stanley may be different in many ways, but they join together and make a difference in their community.

Question Number: 5

Choose the set of words that best describes Stanley.

Ⓐ Solitary and caring
Ⓑ Rude and outgoing
Ⓒ Selfish and quiet
Ⓓ Solitary and rude

Question Number: 6

Based on the passage, how do you think Adam and Stanley feel about one another?

Ⓐ They like and respect one another.
Ⓑ They do not like to spend time together.
Ⓒ They do not enjoy one another's company.
Ⓓ Adam is jealous of Stanley.

Question Number: 7

Choose the set of words that best describes Adam.

Ⓐ Friendly and greedy
Ⓑ Thoughtful and outgoing
Ⓒ Unhappy and mean
Ⓓ Outgoing and greedy

It was the last round of the school spelling bee. Only two students were left. Beau's heart was pounding and he was sweating. He began fidgeting with the button on one of his shirt sleeves.

Question Number: 8

Which adjective describes how Beau was feeling?

Ⓐ anxious
Ⓑ proud
Ⓒ depressed
Ⓓ envious

Libby's grandmother didn't have much money, so she couldn't buy Libby an expensive present for Christmas like her other grandmother could. She didn't want to buy her some cheap toy that wouldn't last long, but she just couldn't afford the things that were on Libby's wish list. She decided that she would make Libby a quilt. She was afraid her granddaughter wouldn't like the gift, but it was the best that she could do.

When Christmas day arrived, Grandmother went to Libby's house. She saw all of the nice gifts that her granddaughter had received. She was worried as Libby began to open her present. Libby squealed with delight when she saw the handmade quilt. She ran and hugged her grandmother and thanked her. She ran and put the new quilt on her bed. The rest of the day she talked about how much she loved the quilt, especially since her grandmother had made it all by hand.

Question Number: 9

How would you describe the way Libby's grandmother felt before Libby opened her gift?

Ⓐ **nervous**
Ⓑ **kind**
Ⓒ **lazy**
Ⓓ **angry**

Question Number: 10

How do you think Libby's grandmother felt after Libby opened the gift?

Ⓐ **sad**
Ⓑ **hungry**
Ⓒ **angry**
Ⓓ **happy**

Describing the Setting (RL.4.3)

Alex the Great

Nearly two thousand five hundred years ago, there lived a king called Alexander the Great. He was the son of Philip II of Macedonia. When Alexander was a boy, a magnificent horse for sale was brought to the court of his father. The animal was to be sold for thirteen talents. Talents are ancient coins. Many were eager to buy the horse, but none could get close enough to saddle the restless animal. He was wild, and it was impossible to ride him.

Alexander pleaded with his father to let him try. Realizing that the horse was terrified of its own shadow, he turned the horse towards the sun so that its shadow fell behind it. This calmed the horse, and the prince proudly rode away. Observing this, his father said, "My son, look for a kingdom worthy of your greatness. Macedonia is too small for you."

That is exactly what Alexander tried to do when he grew up. He fought many battles and always rode Bucephalus. (That was the horse's name.) Friendship and trust grew between man and horse. When Bucephalus died of wounds received in battle, Alexander was heartbroken and deeply mourned the loss of his horse. He wished that he had died along with it.

Question Number: 1

When did this story take place?

Ⓐ **two thousand five hundred years ago**
Ⓑ **two hundred and fifty years ago**
Ⓒ **yesterday**
Ⓓ **It is happening now.**

Fred....dentist

Fred had never been to the dentist. All of his life he had heard horror stories about the buzzing drills, the huge needles, and the scary tools that the dentist used to torture his patients. Since none of his teeth were hurting, Fred just couldn't understand why his mom was insisting on taking him to see one. She told him that it was important to visit the dentist each year and to get your teeth cleaned. That was just silly to Fred since he cleaned his teeth everyday by brushing and flossing them, but nothing would change his mother's mind. He found it hard to believe that she would think it was a good idea to take him somewhere to be tortured. However, he had no choice but to go.

On the way to the dentist, Fred's imagination went wild. He pictured walking into a room with a huge chair that the dentist would strap him to. He could just see the dentist pulling out a huge drill and drilling his tooth while his mother and several others held him in the chair. By the time he got to the dentist's office, he was shaking all over.

To his surprise, the office was nothing like he expected. The dentist was nice, and the chair was comfortable and didn't have any straps with which to tie him to it. He looked around the room and didn't see any huge drills or torture devices. He was relieved when all the dentist did was look

in his mouth, show him how to properly brush and floss his teeth, and give him a balloon. His mom made an appointment to have his teeth cleaned. Maybe this wouldn't be as bad as he had thought it would be.

Question Number: 2

The setting for the second paragraph of the above passage is probably:

Ⓐ **The dentist's office**
Ⓑ **An automobile**
Ⓒ **Fred's home**
Ⓓ **School**

Huckleberry Hound was sitting on the front porch. Suddenly he jumped to his feet and ran through the yard and into the field next to his house. When he got to the field, he put his nose to the ground and started sniffing as he walked. Yep, he definitely smelled a rabbit. He raised his head and howled loudly to let the other dogs know what he had found. Then, he shot after the rabbit like a bolt of lightning. He chased that rabbit for what seemed like hours around that field, but he never caught it. He returned to his yard with his head hanging and his tail tucked between his legs.

Question Number: 3

At the beginning of the story, where was Huckleberry Hound?

Ⓐ **In the yard**
Ⓑ **In a field**
Ⓒ **On the porch**
Ⓓ **In his kennel**

Question Number: 4

Where did Huckleberry Hound chase the rabbit?

Ⓐ **In the yard**
Ⓑ **In a field**
Ⓒ **On the porch**
Ⓓ **In his kennel**

Question Number: 5

Where was Huckleberry Hound at the end of the story?

Ⓐ **In the yard**
Ⓑ **In a field**
Ⓒ **On the porch**
Ⓓ **In his kennel**

I had been craving chocolate ice cream all day. Finally, school was over and I could go get a huge cone of chocolate ice cream. The line was long, but it was worth the wait. The first taste of my ice cream cone was delicious. Then, the worst thing imaginable happened. I bumped into the person behind me and dropped my ice cream on the floor.

Question Number: 6

Where was the writer of the above passage while she was craving chocolate ice cream?

Ⓐ **At home**
Ⓑ **At school**
Ⓒ **At work**
Ⓓ **At the mall**

Question Number: 7

Where was the writer when she dropped her ice cream on the floor?

Ⓐ **At the ice cream shop**
Ⓑ **In the park**
Ⓒ **In her car**
Ⓓ **At home**

"Dad and I need to go out of town this weekend," said Mom. "We'll be back on Monday, so the three of you are going to spend the weekend with your two aunts. "

Lindsay, Scarlet, and Austin loved their aunts and were really excited. They ran upstairs and started getting their things together to take with them. They put everything in one bag that they would have to take to school with them. They were going to stay with Aunt Margaret for two nights and the last night with their Auntie Josephine.

At the end of the school day, the children came running out of classroom doors from all different directions. Aunt Margaret was waiting for her nieces and nephew at the entrance to the school. She was wearing a bright red suit with a sparkly cat pin on it. She also had on a proper wool hat to match. She noticed a scuff on her shoes when her nieces and nephew ran up to her.

She cried, "Oh, my goodness! I am so happy you are here. The children at your school are just a bunch of hooligans. I was nearly trampled while I was standing here! Let's go get in the car." Aunt Margaret pointed to a large, green four-door station wagon parked in the lot.

Question Number: 8

Where does the end of the story take place?

Ⓐ **outside in the yard**
Ⓑ **in the children's bedroom**
Ⓒ **at school**
Ⓓ **at Aunt Margaret's house**

"The Elephant Who Saw the World . . .," Mary started speaking. It was Friday, and they had to share their creative writing stories of the week.

Mary loved writing, and this was her favorite part of the week, when they were able to make up stories for creative writing. She enjoyed it so much that she became really good at it. Even at home on the weekends when she didn't have much homework, she would sit in her room for hours and create stories to share with her friends and family. Her parents always supported her and were her biggest fans.

However, there was one part about every Friday at school that Mary did not enjoy, and that was when she had to share her story in front of the class. The teacher made all of the children share on Friday afternoons, and this made Mary very nervous. She was shy, and although she knew her teacher was right, she didn't like it.

Sitting and listening to the other children, Mary heard her name called. It was her turn to share. She got out of her seat slowly, walked to the front of the room and began.

Question Number: 9

Where does the story take place?

Ⓐ **at Mary's house**
Ⓑ **on the playground at school**
Ⓒ **in Mary's classroom**
Ⓓ **at a restaurant**

It was a beautiful day outside, and a group of children were playing in the yard of one boy's house. They noticed a bee's nest up on the roof, so they started throwing rocks, sticks, and other items trying to knock it down. The nest moved a little, but it didn't fall to the ground. Instead, hundreds of bees flew out going everywhere.

Robert turned and ran away as fast as he could. "Get down! Get down!" he could hear Louise screaming. Robert dove to the ground as many bees flew over him. He could hear all the other kids doing the same.

The bee's nest was still hanging. John looked around the yard for something really long to use. He noticed his dad's rake sitting by the porch, so he took the rake and ran over to the porch. He swung it as hard as he could, hitting the nest. The nest was dislodged, went flying through the air, and landed near Robert. With a shriek, Robert jumped to his feet and ran to the other side of the yard. The others were also yelping and trying to run away.

Question Number: 10

Where does the story take place?

Ⓐ **near a lake**
Ⓑ **outside in the yard**
Ⓒ **in the basement of the house**
Ⓓ **at the school**

Describing Events (RL.4.3)

Timothy

Timothy is a student at my school. He is well liked by all of the teachers and students. We all know that we can count on Timothy to keep our secrets, to help us if we ask, and to always be on time. We know that he is always honest and expects others to be honest as well.

Last summer, Timothy got a job walking dogs each morning. When school started this year, everyone encouraged him to quit his job, but he decided to keep it. He knew it would be hard to get up every morning at 5 a.m. in order to get all of the dogs walked and then go to school all day. In addition, he plans to sing in the chorus, play basketball, and be a mentor in the tutoring program this year. He knows it will not be easy, but he thinks his hard work will be worth it. He is trying to save enough money to go to a youth camp next summer.

Question Number: 1

According to the above passage, Timothy is saving his money for what upcoming event?

Ⓐ **A football game**
Ⓑ **A chorus trip**
Ⓒ **Youth camp**
Ⓓ **A basketball game**

Question Number: 2

Timothy gets up at 5 a.m. every morning to:

Ⓐ **Practice basketball**
Ⓑ **Walk dogs**
Ⓒ **Do his homework**
Ⓓ **Tutor a classmate**

Fred....dentist

Fred had never been to the dentist. All of his life he had heard horror stories about the buzzing drills, the huge needles, and the scary tools that the dentist used to torture his patients. Since none of his teeth were hurting, Fred just couldn't understand why his mom was insisting on taking him to see one. She told him that it was important to visit the dentist each year and to get your teeth cleaned. That was just silly to Fred since he cleaned his teeth everyday by brushing and flossing them, but nothing would change his mother's mind. He found it hard to believe that she would think it was a good idea to take him somewhere to be tortured. However, he had no choice but to go.

On the way to the dentist, Fred's imagination went wild. He pictured walking into a room with a huge chair that the dentist would strap him to. He could just see the dentist pulling out a huge drill and drilling his tooth while his mother and several others held him in the chair. By the time he got to the dentist's office, he was shaking all over.

To his surprise, the office was nothing like he expected. The dentist was nice and the chair was comfortable and didn't have any straps with which to tie him to it. He looked around the room and didn't see any huge drills or torture devices. All the dentist did was look in his mouth, show him how to properly brush and floss his teeth, and give him a balloon. His mom made an appointment to have his teeth cleaned. Maybe this wouldn't be as bad as he had thought it would be.

Question Number: 3

Which detail shows that Fred is worried about going to the dentist?

Ⓐ **To his surprise, the office was nothing like he expected.**
Ⓑ **Since none of his teeth were hurting, Fred just couldn't understand why his mom was insisting on taking him to see one.**
Ⓒ **By the time he got to the dentist he was shaking all over**
Ⓓ **Maybe this wouldn't be as bad as he thought it would be.**

Question Number: 4

What did Fred imagine was going to happen to him at the dentist office?

Ⓐ **The dentist would pull a tooth and then give him a balloon.**
Ⓑ **The dentist would tie him to the chair and use a huge drill on him.**
Ⓒ **His mother would hold him down, and the dentist would clean his teeth.**
Ⓓ **The dentist would tie him down and floss his teeth.**

Question Number: 5

What actually happened at the dentist office?

Ⓐ **The dentist showed him how to brush and floss his teeth.**
Ⓑ **The dentist pulled a tooth.**
Ⓒ **The dentist drilled his tooth.**
Ⓓ **The dentist pulled a tooth and gave him a balloon.**

Adam lives with his dad and his older brother Stanley. Adam and Stanley share a room. Most of the time Adam enjoys sharing a room with his brother, but there are times that he wished he had his own room. Being brothers, they have a lot in common; however, they are different in many ways.

Adam likes to spend time with his friends. If he is not with them, he is texting them or playing games with them online. Adam is always busy. He cannot stand to sit around and do nothing. In fact, the only time he is still is when he is sleeping. Adam plays football, basketball, soccer, and baseball. He loves to be involved in whatever is going on at school or at the town's youth center. He spends a lot of his time encouraging people to recycle and even volunteers at the youth center. Although he loves spending time with his friends, he is willing to give up time with them to help others.

Stanley, on the other hand, loves to stay at home. He enjoys activities that can be done alone such as reading, drawing, and spending time with his dogs. Most days after school you can find him at home enjoying one of his favorite activities. He also thinks recycling is important and makes sure his family does it. Although he likes being alone, he enjoys volunteering at the youth center with his brother. He thinks it is important to make a difference in the lives of others, which is why he thinks he would like to be a doctor. Adam and Stanley may be different in many ways, but they join together and make a difference in their community.

Question Number: 6

According to the passage above, what do Adam and Stanley enjoy doing together?

Ⓐ **Playing football**
Ⓑ **Drawing cartoons**
Ⓒ **Playing video games**
Ⓓ **Volunteering at the youth center**

"The Elephant Who Saw the World . . .," Mary started speaking. It was Friday, and they had to share their creative writing stories of the week.

Mary loved writing, and this was her favorite part of the week, when they were able to make up stories for creative writing. She enjoyed it so much that she became really good at it. Even at home on the weekends when she didn't have much homework, she would sit in her room for hours and create stories to share with her friends and family. Her parents always supported her and were her biggest fans.

However, there was one part about every Friday at school that Mary did not enjoy, and that was when she had to share her story in front of the class. The teacher made all of the children share on Friday afternoons, and this made Mary very nervous. She was shy, and although she knew her teacher was right, she didn't like it.

Sitting and listening to the other children, Mary heard her name called. It was her turn to share. She got out of her seat slowly, walked to the front of the room and began.

Question Number: 7

Which event in the above paragraph made Mary nervous?

Ⓐ **writing a story**
Ⓑ **talking to the teacher**
Ⓒ **sharing her work in front of the class**
Ⓓ **showing her family what she had done**

"Dad and I need to go out of town this weekend," said Mom. "We'll be back on Monday, so the three of you are going to spend the weekend with your two aunts. "

Lindsay, Scarlet, and Austin loved their aunts and were really excited. They ran upstairs and started getting their things together to take with them. They put everything in one bag that they would have to take to school with them. They were going to stay with Aunt Margaret for two nights and the last night with their Auntie Josephine.

At the end of the school day, the children came running out of classroom doors from all different directions. Aunt Margaret was waiting for her nieces and nephew at the entrance of the school. She was wearing a bright red suit with a sparkly cat pin on it. She also had on a proper wool hat to match. She noticed a scuff on her shoes when her nieces and nephew ran up to her.

She cried, "Oh, my goodness! I am so happy you are here. The children at your school are just a bunch of hooligans. I was nearly trampled while I was standing here! Let's go get in the car." Aunt Margaret pointed to a large, green four-door station wagon parked in the lot.

Question Number: 8

What most likely happened to Aunt Margaret while she was waiting for her nieces and nephew?

Ⓐ **The children ambushed her while she was waiting in the parking lot.**
Ⓑ **She was in a bad mood already and called the children "hooligans" for no reason.**
Ⓒ **Mean spirited children knocked her down because she was a stranger.**
Ⓓ **The school children were excited school was out and they bumped into her in their hurry to get to their homes and after school activities.**

Question Number: 9

Why did the children need to stay with their two aunts?

Ⓐ **Their parents needed to hang decorations around the house.**
Ⓑ **Their parents were celebrating their anniversary.**
Ⓒ **Their parents needed to go out of town.**
Ⓓ **Their parents neeeded to helping her little brother Austin go shopping for school.**

Read the two passages and answer the question that follow.

Passage 1

"The Elephant Who Saw the World . . . " Mary started speaking. It was Friday, and they had to share their creative writing stories of the week.

Mary loved writing, and this was her favorite part of the week, when they were able to make up stories for creative writing. She enjoyed it so much that she became really good at it. Even at home on the weekends when she didn't have much homework, she would sit in her room for hours

and create stories to share with her friends and family. Her parents always supported her and were her biggest fans.

However, there was one part about every Friday at school that Mary did not enjoy, and that was when she had to share her story in front of the class. The teacher made all of the children share on Friday afternoons, and this made Mary very nervous. She was shy, and although she knew her teacher was right, she didn't like it.

Sitting and listening to the other children, Mary heard her name called. It was her turn to share. She got out of her seat slowly, walked to the front of the room and began.

Passage 2

Timmy grabbed his paper and ran to the front of the classroom. Today was the day! He was so excited to finally have a chance to tell his story. He loved writing and his mind swam with ideas but he couldn't seem to get them all out. For weeks, he had worked and worked so hard to get the right words down on the page.

Finally, during writing time this week, his ideas gelled and the words flowed, creating the most exciting piece of work possible. His story was sure to capture the minds of his classmates and they would want him to tell stories again and again. He was even ready to read the story aloud, having practiced different voices for the different characters and parts of the story.

As he sat and listened to the other children, he bubbled over with excitement and anticipation. Hearing his name, he jumped up and ran to the front of the classroom. "Long ago," Timmy began, "a spaceship came and landed on my grandfather's barn..."

Question Number: 10

Which choices below accurately describe Mary and Timmy's feelings about presenting to the class?

Ⓐ **Mary loved writing; Timmy struggled to get the words right.**
Ⓑ **Timmy loved writing; Mary struggled to get the words right.**
Ⓒ **Mary was shy; Timmy was very excited.**
Ⓓ **Timmy was shy; Mary was very excited.**

Figurative Language (RL.4.4)

Question Number: 1

Her eyes twinkled like diamonds as she looked lovingly at her new kitten.
Identify the simile used in the above sentence.

Ⓐ her eyes twinkled
Ⓑ as she looked lovingly
Ⓒ at her new kitten
Ⓓ twinkled like diamonds

Question Number: 2

Elaine has no sympathy for others. You know she has a heart of stone.
Identify the metaphor in the above passage.

Ⓐ no sympathy for others
Ⓑ a heart of stone
Ⓒ no sympathy
Ⓓ she has a heart

Question Number: 3

Identify the sentence that contains a metaphor.

Ⓐ She is as sweet as sugar.
Ⓑ She is as blind as a bat.
Ⓒ The sound of the chirping birds is music to my ears.
Ⓓ Billy is as stubborn as a mule.

Question Number: 4

Suzy eats like a bird.
This simile means that Suzy:

Ⓐ eats nuts and seeds
Ⓑ eats many large meals
Ⓒ eats while flying
Ⓓ eats very little

Question Number: 5

My wife is my compass that guides me to the correct paths in life.
The metaphor in the above passage compares his wife to:

Ⓐ a passage
Ⓑ compass
Ⓒ a guide
Ⓓ life

Question Number: 6

I really got a bad deal on the used car I bought. That <u>car was a real lemon</u>.
The metaphor in this passage is used to let you know that the car:

Ⓐ was a good buy
Ⓑ had a very low price
Ⓒ was yellow
Ⓓ didn't run well

Question Number: 7

Choose the sentence that contains a simile.

Ⓐ Your room is a pig pen. How do you even find your bed?
Ⓑ It has rained cats and dogs all day long. I wish the rain would stop.
Ⓒ Our math home work was a breeze.
Ⓓ I could not eat Susan's biscuits because they were as hard as a rock.

Question Number: 8

Janice is such an angel means that Janice is:

Ⓐ mean
Ⓑ annoying
Ⓒ kind
Ⓓ has wings

Question Number: 9

Jimmy is an ox.
The metaphor is an ox means what?

Ⓐ He is weak.
Ⓑ He is blind.
Ⓒ He is strong.
Ⓓ He is deaf.

Question Number: 10

Linda is a road hog. She drives too fast.
What is the metaphor in the sentence above?

Ⓐ She drives too fast.
Ⓑ She is a road hog.
Ⓒ Linda
Ⓓ None of the above

Text Structure (RL.4.5)

Question Number: 1

Which text structure is used in the classic story "The Three Little Pigs?"

Ⓐ **Cause and effect**
Ⓑ **Compare and contrast**
Ⓒ **Problem and solution**
Ⓓ **Sequence or chronological**

I saw the most unusual chair in a furniture store today while walking around the mall. The chair was shaped like a high-heel shoe. The seat was created from the toe of the shoe, and the high heel and back of the shoe created the chair's back. Hot pink velvet covered the top portion of the shoe chair. Black velvet covered the bottom and heel of the shoe chair. Along the sides of the toes and heel, huge rhinestones were glued onto the velvet. I wonder who would want a chair like that.

Question Number: 2

What is the structure of the above text?

Ⓐ **Cause and effect**
Ⓑ **Compare and contrast**
Ⓒ **Problem and solution**
Ⓓ **Description**

"Dad and I need to go out of town this weekend," said Mom. "We'll be back on Monday, so the three of you are going to spend the weekend with your two aunts. "

Lindsay, Scarlet, and Austin loved their aunts and were really excited. They ran upstairs and started getting their things together to take with them. They put everything in one bag that they would have to take to school with them. They were going to stay with Aunt Margaret for two nights and the last night with their Auntie Josephine.

At the end of the school day, the children came running out of classroom doors from all different directions. Aunt Margaret was waiting for her nieces and nephew at the entrance to the school. She was wearing a bright red suit with a sparkly cat pin on it. She also had on a proper wool hat to match. She noticed a scuff on her shoes when her nieces and nephew ran up to her.

She cried, "Oh, my goodness! I am so happy you are here. The children at your school are just a bunch of hooligans. I was nearly trampled while I was standing here! Let's go get in the car." Aunt Margaret pointed to a large, green four-door station wagon parked in the lot.

Question Number: 3

What is the structure of the above text?

Ⓐ a play
Ⓑ a comedy
Ⓒ a poem
Ⓓ a narrative

Before going to bed on Friday night, Susie's parents told her they had a surprise planned for the weekend and she would have to wake up really early on Saturday morning. When she woke up, they left the house quickly and started driving. While in the car, Susie looked outside to see if she could figure out where they were going. She noticed that it was getting really hot out and the sun was shining brightly. Then she noticed that the surfboards were in the car. Finally, they stopped, and Susie said, "I know where we are going!"

Question Number: 4

What is the structure of the text?

Ⓐ **Cause and Effect**
Ⓑ **Problem and Solution**
Ⓒ **Sequencing and Chronological**
Ⓓ **Description**

One day James went to town to buy new clothes. First, he tried on a pair of trousers. He didn't like the trousers, so he gave them back to the shopkeeper. Then, he tried on a robe which had the same price as the trousers. James was pleased with the robe, and he left the shop. Before he climbed on his donkey to ride home, the shopkeeper and the shop-assistant ran out.

Question Number: 5

What is the structure of the above text?

Ⓐ **Descriptive**
Ⓑ **Problem and Solution**
Ⓒ **Cause and Effect**
Ⓓ **Sequencing and Chronological**

Beau was a nine-year-old boy who wanted a pet dog very badly. Every day, he asked his parents for a dog. They always told him no, because they didn't think he was responsible enough to take care of a dog. One day, Beau made a deal with his parents. He told them that he would keep his room clean and do other household chores for an entire month to prove he was responsible enough to have a pet. That is exactly what he did, and his parents got him a fluffy, white puppy he named Snow White.

Question Number: 6

What is the text structure of this passage?

Ⓐ **Description**
Ⓑ **Cause and Effect**
Ⓒ **Compare/Contrast**
Ⓓ **Problem/Solution**

Read the two passages and answer the questions that follow.

Passage 1

"The Elephant Who Saw the World . . . " Mary started speaking. It was Friday, and they had to share their creative writing stories of the week.

Mary loved writing, and this was her favorite part of the week, when they were able to make up stories for creative writing. She enjoyed it so much that she became really good at it. Even at home on the weekends when she didn't have much homework, she would sit in her room for hours and create stories to share with her friends and family. Her parents always supported her and were her biggest fans.

However, there was one part about every Friday at school that Mary did not enjoy, and that was when she had to share her story in front of the class. The teacher made all of the children share on Friday afternoons, and this made Mary very nervous. She was shy, and although she knew her teacher was right, she didn't like it.

Sitting and listening to the other children, Mary heard her name called. It was her turn to share. She got out of her seat slowly, walked to the front of the room and began.

Passage 2

Timmy grabbed his paper and ran to the front of the classroom. Today was the day! He was so excited to finally have a chance to tell his story. He loved writing and his mind swam with ideas but he couldn't seem to get them all out. For weeks, he had worked and worked so hard to get the right words down on the page.

Finally, during writing time this week, his ideas gelled and the words flowed, creating the most exciting piece of work possible. His story was sure to capture the minds of his classmates and they would want him to tell stories again and again. He was even ready to read the story aloud, having practiced different voices for the different characters and parts of the story.

As he sat and listened to the other children, he bubbled over with excitement and anticipation. Hearing his name, he jumped up and ran to the front of the classroom. "Long ago," Timmy be-gan, "a spaceship came and landed on my grandfather's barn..."

Question Number: 7

How does the description of Mary and Timmy add to the setting of the story?

Ⓐ Describing their emotions and feelings allows the reader to connect with both characters.
Ⓑ Describing their thoughts needs more dialogue.
Ⓒ The words and phrases the author uses deepens the description of the classroom.
Ⓓ The descriptions allow the reader to see that Timmy is too shy to read his story but does it anyway.

When I was little my mom gave me a diary. She told me that it was something really personal and special since we can use it to write down all our thoughts and ideas.

Some famous people have kept diaries and when they died, their diary was published into a book. Someone now famous who kept a diary of her thoughts was Anne Frank. Anne Frank lived during the time of World War II in the Netherlands; however, she was originally from Germany. During the time of the second World War, a political group called the Nazis were in power in Germany and they did not like Jews. Anne and her family were Jewish which is why they left Germany for the Netherlands when Anne was very young.

While they were in the Netherlands, they were in hiding from the Nazis. Anne's family had to hide in someone's attic for two years and one month so they could stay safe. Since Anne couldn't do much outside of the attic except go to school, she kept a diary and wrote down all her thoughts about what was happening to her and her family.

Question Number: 8

What is the structure of this text?

Ⓐ Chronological
Ⓑ Cause and Effect
Ⓒ Descriptive
Ⓓ Problem and Solution

This year Jim and I had the most wonderful vacation compared to the one we took last year. This year Jim and I went to Hawaii, which is a much better place to visit than a hunting lodge in Alaska. The hotel we stayed in was a luxury suite. It included a big screen TV with all of the movie channels, a hot tub on the balcony, a small kitchen stocked with local fruits and vegetables, and a huge bed shaped like a pineapple. The weather in Hawaii could not have been any better. We enjoyed many hours on the beach sunbathing and playing volleyball. When we were not on the beach, we were in the ocean swimming or riding the waves on a surf board. Each night we enjoyed eating and dancing with all of our friends at a luau. Our week in Hawaii rushed by, making us wish we had planned a two-week vacation.

On a different note, the hunting lodge in Alaska had no TV, a shower with barely warm water, a small cooler for our food, and cots to sleep on each night. The room wasn't even the worst part of the vacation. The weather was terrible. It rained the entire time we were there. Even with the rain, our guide expected us to go on the all-day fishing trip that was part of our vacation package. All we caught on that fishing trip was a cold from the rain. After the third day, we decided to cut our trip short and head for home. Without a doubt, we will be going back to Hawaii next year on our vacation.

Question Number: 9

Choose the text structure used in this passage.

Ⓐ **Cause and effect**
Ⓑ **Compare and contrast**
Ⓒ **Problem and solution**
Ⓓ **Sequence**

A lesson in your science book has a story of a young boy catching a sickness by germs that were spread and discusses how germs are spread. He has to see a doctor who shows him how to avoid sickness happening again in the future.

Question Number: 10

What is the structure of the above text?

Ⓐ **Cause and effect**
Ⓑ **Compare and contrast**
Ⓒ **Problem and solution**
Ⓓ **Sequence or chronological**

Point of View (RL.4.6)

You are not the kind of guy who would be at a place like this at this time of the morning. But here you are, and you cannot say that the terrain is entirely unfamiliar, although the details are fuzzy.
—Opening lines of Jay McInerney's Bright Lights, Big City (1984)

Question Number: 1

The above passage uses which style of narration?

Ⓐ **First person**
Ⓑ **Second person**
Ⓒ **Third person**
Ⓓ **Fourth person**

I was so scared when I first learned that I would be having my tooth pulled. I didn't sleep at all the night before the procedure. I was terrified that it would hurt more than I could bear. I was shaking like a leaf when I sat in the dentist chair. He promised me that it would not hurt, but I certainly had my doubts. The dentist then gave me some medicine. When I awoke, my tooth was gone and I didn't remember a thing.

Question Number: 2

The above passage uses which style of narration?

Ⓐ **First person**
Ⓑ **Second person**
Ⓒ **Third person**
Ⓓ **Fourth person**

Huckleberry Hound ran through the yard and into the field next to his house. Suddenly, he put his nose to the ground and started sniffing as he walked. Yep, he definitely smelled a rabbit. He raised his head and howled loudly to let the other dogs know what he had found. Then, he shot after the rabbit like a bolt of lightning. He chased that rabbit for what seemed like hours, but he never caught it. He returned to his yard with his head hanging and his tail tucked between his legs.

Question Number: 3

The above passage uses which style of narration?

Ⓐ **First person**
Ⓑ **Second person**
Ⓒ **Third person**
Ⓓ **Fourth person**

You didn't want to ask for a loan, but you had no choice. You spent all of your allowance at the ballgame, and now you don't have the money to buy your mom a birthday present.

Question Number: 4

The above passage uses which style of narration?

Ⓐ **First person**
Ⓑ **Second person**
Ⓒ **Third person**
Ⓓ **Fourth person**

Max went for a ride in the park. While on his ride, he saw his best friend. They decided to go to the movies instead of riding in the park. Max called his mom and asked if it would be alright to go to the movie with his friend. She said yes, so Max and Sammy jumped on their bikes and went to see *Superman*.

Question Number: 5

The above passage uses which style of narration?

Ⓐ **First person**
Ⓑ **Second person**
Ⓒ **Third person**
Ⓓ **Fourth person**

I had been craving chocolate ice cream all day. Finally, school was over and I could go get a huge cone of chocolate ice cream. The line was long, but it was worth the wait. The first taste of my ice cream cone was delicious. Then, the worst thing imaginable happened. I bumped into the person behind me and dropped my ice cream on the floor.

Question Number: 6

The above passage uses which style of narration?

Ⓐ **First person**
Ⓑ **Second person**
Ⓒ **Third person**
Ⓓ **Fourth person**

I wanted to learn how to knit, so I asked my grandmother to teach me. She agreed, so I went to the store and bought yarn and knitting needles. I had my first lesson last week. I quickly learned that knitting is much harder than I thought it would be. I don't think I want to learn to knit anymore.

Question Number: 7

The above passage uses which style of narration?

Ⓐ **First person**
Ⓑ **Second person**
Ⓒ **Third person**
Ⓓ **Fourth person**

I wonder why Mindy didn't come to the meeting. Did I forget to tell her about? Did she forget about it? I think I will call her and see why she isn't here.

Question Number: 8

The above passage uses which style of narration?

Ⓐ **First person**
Ⓑ **Second person**
Ⓒ **Third person**
Ⓓ **Fourth person**

Opal walked into the store not wanting to do what she had planned. She knew when she took the makeup without paying for it that it was wrong. She felt so guilty. She knew she couldn't keep the makeup. So, gathering all of her courage, she walked up to the security officer and confessed what she had done.

Question Number: 9

The above passage uses which style of narration?

Ⓐ **First person**
Ⓑ **Second person**
Ⓒ **Third person**
Ⓓ **Fourth person**

One day James went to town to buy new clothes. First, he tried on a pair of trousers. He didn't like the trousers, so he gave them back to the shopkeeper. Then he tried on a robe, which had the same price as the trousers. James was pleased with the robe, and he left the shop. Before he climbed on his donkey to ride home, the shopkeeper and the shop-assistant ran out.

Question Number: 10

What style of narration is the above text?

Ⓐ **First person**
Ⓑ **Second person**
Ⓒ **Third person**
Ⓓ **Fourth person**

Visual Connections (RL.4.7)

"The Elephant Who Saw the World . . . " Mary started speaking. It was Friday, and they had to share their creative writing stories of the week.

Mary loved writing, and this was her favorite part of the week, when they were able to make up stories for creative writing. She enjoyed it so much that she became really good at it. Even at home on the weekends when she didn't have much homework, she would sit in her room for hours and create stories to share with her friends and family. Her parents always supported her and were her biggest fans.

However, there was one part about every Friday at school that Mary did not enjoy, and that was when she had to share her story in front of the class. The teacher made all of the children share on Friday afternoons, and this made Mary very nervous. She was shy, and although she knew her teacher was right, she didn't like it.

Sitting and listening to the other children, Mary heard her name called. It was her turn to share. She got out of her seat slowly, walked to the front of the room and began.

Question Number: 1

Which picture below best represents what's happening in the story?

Ⓓ **None of the above**

Question Number: 2

Which text below best represents what is happening in the picture?

Ⓐ Thelma watched her two baby lions, Louis and Lisa as they played. They were playing well until they started fighting over something the zoo keeper had thrown into the enclosure. Living at a zoo was pretty boring. They didn't have much room to move around and explore. The baby lions often got into trouble because they were tired of doing the same thing, and they would then get really destructive -- once they destroyed a fuzzy ball they were given and knocked over their water dish many times. The visitors of the zoo who saw what was happening thought it was really funny!

Ⓑ Thelma watched her two baby meerkats, Louis and Lisa, as they played. They were playing well until they started fighting over something the zoo keeper had thrown into the enclosure. Living at a zoo was pretty boring. They didn't have much room to move around and explore. The baby meerkats often got into trouble because they were tired of doing the same thing, and they would then get really destructive -- once they destroyed a fuzzy ball they were given and knocked over their water dish many times. The visitors of the zoo who saw what was happening thought it was really funny!

Ⓒ Thelma watched her two baby monkeys, Louis and Lisa, as they played. They were playing well until they started fighting over something the zoo keeper had thrown into the enclosure. Living at a zoo was pretty boring. They didn't have much room to move around and explore. The baby monkeys often got into trouble because they were tired of doing the same thing. They would then get really destructive! Once they destroyed a fuzzy ball they were given and knocked over their water dish many times. The visitors of the zoo who saw what was happening thought it was really funny!

Ⓓ **None of the above**

Question Number: 3

Which paragraph would be an appropriate description for the picture above?

(A) One day last spring I was out walking as it was a beautiful spring day. I came across an empty forest and heard a noise. It sounded like a baby but it couldn't have been a baby since there was no one else there. I walked over to where I thought the noise was coming from and stopped in front of a large hollow tree. It looked as if it had been there for a very long time. I stopped and listened. I heard the noise again and it was definitely coming from inside the tree. I looked inside and I saw a little kitten. At first the kitten was scared but eventually, with lots of coaxing, came to the opening of a hole in the tree. I was able to see that it was a little grey kitten who was probably very hungry and scared. I took the kitten home and it became my companion from that day on.

(B) One day last spring I was out walking as it was a beautiful spring day. I came across an empty parking lot and heard a noise. It sounded like a baby but it couldn't have been a baby since there was no one else there. I walked over to where I thought the noise was coming from and stopped in front of a large box. It looked like some thing someone may have used for moving. I stopped and listened. I heard the noise again and it was definitely coming from inside the box. I looked inside and I saw a little kitten. At first the kitten was scared but eventually, with lots of coaxing, came to the open end of the box. I was able to see that it was a little black and white kitten who was probably very hungry and scared. I took the kitten home and it became my companion from that day on.

(C) One day last spring I was out walking as it was a beautiful spring day. I came across a construction site and heard a noise. It sounded like a baby but it couldn't have been a baby since there was no one else there. I walked over to where I thought the noise was coming from and stopped in front of a large cement pipe. It looked like some thing they might use to transport water underground. I stopped and listened. I heard the noise again and it was definitely coming from inside the pipe. I looked inside and I saw a little kitten. At first the kitten was scared but eventually, with lots of coaxing, came to one of the open ends of the pipe. I was able to see that it was a little black and white kitten who was probably very hungry and scared. I took the kitten home and it became my companion from that day on.

(D) **None of the above**

Question Number: 4

Which of the statements below most accurately reflects the picture?

Ⓐ   **Many people like to act, even if they don't act very well. Acting helps them express how they are feeling. Sometimes acting makes them feel happy. Not everyone wants to be a professional, though. Professional actors like to entertain other people. Their skill is usually a combination of talent and training. Most professional actors work with a coach. They usually start acting when they are young. Many of them get their first experience by being in school musicals or plays. Talent and training are not enough to make a successful career, though. Young people who want to be actors should also have poise, good stage presence, creativity, and the ability to deal with change.**

Ⓑ   **Many people like to dance, even if they don't dance very well. Dancing helps them express how they are feeling. Sometimes dancing makes them feel happy. Not every one wants to be a professional, though. Professional dancers like to entertain other people. Their skill is usually a combination of talent and training. Most professional dancers work with a coach. They usually start training at a young age. Many of them get their first experience by being in school musicals. Talent and training are not enough to make a successful career, though. Young people who want to be dancers should also have poise, good stage presence, creativity, and the ability to deal with change. They must be healthy and strong, too.**

Ⓒ   **Many people like to sing, even if they don't sing very well. Singing helps them express how they are feeling. Sometimes singing makes them feel happy. Not everyone wants to be a professional, though. Professional singers use their voices to entertain other people. Their skill is usually a combination of talent and training. Most professional singers work with a coach. They usually start training when their voices are mature. Many of them get their first experience by being in school musicals or choirs. Talent and training are not enough to make a successful career, though. Young people who want to be singers should also have poise, good stage presence, creativity, and the ability to deal with change. They must be healthy and strong, too. There is a lot of travel, and performance schedules are not regular. Singers have to be on their game when they perform.**

Ⓓ   **None of the above**

Question Number: 5

Which paragraph would be an appropriate description for the picture above?

Ⓐ Summer is probably my favorite season. One of my most favorite things to do is to go watch a sandcastle building contest they have every year in San Diego, California. We can see amazing sandcastles that people spend hours and days building. This year one of the winners of the contest made this really large superhero to honor their love of comic books.

Ⓑ Summer is probably my favorite season. One of my most favorite things to do is to go watch a sandcastle building contest they have every year in San Diego, California. We can see amazing sandcastles that people spend hours and days building. This year one of the winners of the contest made this really long snake to honor their Mexican heritage.

Ⓒ Summer is probably my favorite season. One of my most favorite things to do is to go watch a sandcastle building contest they have every year in San Diego, California. We can see amazing sandcastles that people spend hours and days building. This year one of the winners of the contest made this really big pyramid to honor their Egyptian heritage.

Ⓓ Summer is probably my favorite season. One of my most favorite things to do is to go watch a sandcastle building contest they have every year in San Diego, California. We can see amazing sandcastles that people spend hours and days building. This year one of the winners of the contest made this really long dragon to honor their Chinese heritage.

"Good morning boys and girls," said Mrs. Miller. "We are going to try something new today. It is called Echo Reading. This is a new reading strategy for our class. During reading time, I will read aloud two or three sentences while you follow along silently. Then, you will read aloud the same sentences I just read."

Question Number: 6

What would be an important picture or illustration to use with this paragraph?

Ⓐ **a book**
Ⓑ **a teacher and student looking at the same book**
Ⓒ **a classroom full of students**
Ⓓ **a pencil and paper**

The Man, the Hawk, and the Dove

LONG AGO IN NIGERIA, there was a man who had been blind and lame all his life. One evening, as he was sitting in front of his house, he couldn't help but feel sorry for himself. After all, he couldn't walk or see.

All of a sudden, a dove flew into his robe.

"Save me," the dove whispered urgently.

Then a hawk whished up and stopped in front of the man. "This dove is mine," squawked the hawk.

The man gripped the robe tightly.

"I beg you, you don't know how terribly hungry I am," said the hawk. "If I don't have that dove, I will die. I am a hawk and you know that we must eat what we can." Then he straightened up and said, "Hawks see for miles around. If you release the dove to me, I'll share the secret of how your eyesight can be restored."

The man hesitated. After all, wasn't it true that the basic nature of all things is that one beast hunts another?

"You mustn't listen to that hawk!" chirped the dove frantically. "If you save me from certain death, I'll tell you how your legs can be healed so you can walk."

What was he to do? Fortunately, the footsteps of his best friend were approaching.

"Should I gain my sight, or my legs?" he asked his friend.

The friend was silent. "Well," he said at last, "you have to paddle your own canoe. I can't help you decide this one."

"The next time you ask, I'll be sure to give you good advice, too!" the man called out as his friend walked quickly away.

Question Number: 7

What image would help the reader understand the moral of the fable?

Ⓐ **The dove flying into the man's coat**
Ⓑ **The hawk talking to the man**
Ⓒ **The man talking to his friend**
Ⓓ **The friend walking away from the man**

Question Number: 8

What caption would best help the readers understand the image above from Treasure Island?

Ⓐ **"Livesey," returned the squire, "you are always in the right of it. I'll be as silent as the grave."**
Ⓑ **The doctor opened the seals with great care, and there fell out the map of an island**
Ⓒ **I said good-bye to Mother and the cove, and the dear old Admiral Benbow**
Ⓓ **On our little walk along the quays, he made himself the most interesting companion**

Read the two passages and answer the questions that follow.

Passage 1

"The Elephant Who Saw the World . . . " Mary started speaking. It was Friday, and they had to share their creative writing stories of the week.

Mary loved writing, and this was her favorite part of the week, when they were able to make up stories for creative writing. She enjoyed it so much that she became really good at it. Even at home on the weekends when she didn't have much homework, she would sit in her room for hours and

create stories to share with her friends and family. Her parents always supported her and were her biggest fans.

However, there was one part about every Friday at school that Mary did not enjoy, and that was when she had to share her story in front of the class. The teacher made all of the children share on Friday afternoons, and this made Mary very nervous. She was shy, and although she knew her teacher was right, she didn't like it.

Sitting and listening to the other children, Mary heard her name called. It was her turn to share. She got out of her seat slowly, walked to the front of the room and began.

Passage 2

Timmy grabbed his paper and ran to the front of the classroom. Today was the day! He was so excited to finally have a chance to tell his story. He loved writing and his mind swam with ideas but he couldn't seem to get them all out. For weeks, he had worked and worked so hard to get the right words down on the page.

Finally, during writing time this week, his ideas gelled and the words flowed, creating the most exciting piece of work possible. His story was sure to capture the minds of his classmates and they would want him to tell stories again and again. He was even ready to read the story aloud, having practiced different voices for the different characters and parts of the story.

As he sat and listened to the other children, he bubbled over with excitement and anticipation. Hearing his name, he jumped up and ran to the front of the classroom. "Long ago," Timmy began, "a spaceship came and landed on my grandfather's barn…"

Question Number: 9

If you were to create a Venn Diagram of Mary's and Timmy's experiences with their writing assignment, what would go in the intersecting circle?

- Ⓐ **Loved writing**
- Ⓑ **Did not want to share with class**
- Ⓒ **Could not wait to share with class**
- Ⓓ **Wrote a fiction story**

Timmy grabbed his paper and ran to the front of the classroom. Today was the day! He was so excited to finally have a chance to tell his story. He loved writing and his mind swam with ideas but he couldn't seem to get them all out. For weeks, he had worked and worked so hard to get the right words down on the page.

Finally, during writing time this week, his ideas gelled and the words flowed, creating the most exciting piece of work possible. His story was sure to capture the minds of his classmates and they would want him to tell stories again and again. He was even ready to read the story aloud, having practiced different voices for the different characters and parts of the story.

As he sat and listened to the other children, he bubbled over with excitement and anticipation. Hearing his name, he jumped up and ran to the front of the classroom. "Long ago," Timmy began, "a spaceship came and landed on my grandfather's barn..."

Question Number: 10

What image could Timmy include to add depth to his story?

Ⓐ

Ⓑ

Ⓒ

Ⓓ

Comparing and Contrasting (RL.4.9)

Fred....dentist

Fred had never been to the dentist. All of his life he had heard horror stories about the buzzing drills, the huge needles, and the scary tools that the dentist used to torture his patients. Since none of his teeth were hurting, Fred just couldn't understand why his mom was insisting on taking him to see one. She told him that it was important to visit the dentist each year and to get your teeth cleaned. That was just silly to Fred since he cleaned his teeth everyday by brushing and flossing them, but nothing would change his mother's mind. He found it hard to believe that she would think it was a good idea to take him somewhere to be tortured. However, he had no choice but to go.

On the way to the dentist, Fred's imagination went wild. He pictured walking into a room with a huge chair that the dentist would strap him to. He could just see the dentist pulling out a huge drill and drilling his tooth while his mother and several others held him in the chair. By the time he got to the dentist's office, he was shaking all over.

To his surprise, the office was nothing like he expected. The dentist was nice and the chair was comfortable and didn't have any straps with which to tie him to it. He looked around the room and didn't see any huge drills or torture devices. He was relieved when all the dentist did was look in his mouth, show him how to properly brush and floss his teeth, and give him a balloon. His mom made an appointment to have his teeth cleaned. Maybe this wouldn't be as bad as he had thought it would be.

Question Number: 1

Compare the way Fred felt about going to the dentist before his visit to the way he felt after his first visit.

Ⓐ **Fred was excited about going but became afraid once he arrived.**
Ⓑ **Fred was afraid of going and was even more afraid after he met the dentist.**
Ⓒ **Fred was afraid of going but felt relieved after he met the dentist.**
Ⓓ **Fred was excited about going and loved it once he arrived.**

Read all three passages and answer the questions that follow

Passage 1:

Timothy

Timothy got a job walking dogs each morning. When school started this year, everyone encouraged him to quit his job, but he decided to keep it. He knew it would be hard to get up every morning at 5 a.m. in order to get all of the dogs walked and then go to school all day. In addition, he plans to sing in the chorus, play basketball, and be a mentor in the tutoring program this year. He knows it will not be easy, but he thinks his hard work will be worth it. He is trying to save enough money to go to a youth camp next summer.

Passage 2:

Adam likes to spend time with his friends. If he is not with them, he is texting them or playing games with them online. Adam is always busy. He cannot stand to sit around and do nothing. In fact, the only time he is still is when he is sleeping. Adam plays football, basketball, soccer, and baseball. He loves to be involved in whatever is going on at school or at the town's youth center. He spends a lot of his time encouraging people to recycle and even volunteers at the youth center. Although he loves spending time with his friends, he is willing to give up time with them to help others.

Passage 3

Stanley loves to stay at home. He enjoys activities that can be done alone such as reading, drawing, and spending time with his dogs. Most days after school you can find him at home enjoying one of his favorite activities. He also thinks recycling is important and makes sure his family does it. Although he likes being alone, he enjoys volunteering at the youth center with his brother. He thinks it is important to make a difference in the lives others, which is why he thinks he would like to be a doctor. Adam and Stanley may be different in many ways, but they join together and make a difference in their community.

Question Number: 2

If you compare and contrast Timothy and Adam, which statement is correct?

Ⓐ **Timothy participates in extracurricular activities, but Adam does not.**
Ⓑ **Timothy does not participate in extracurricular activities, but Adam does.**
Ⓒ **Timothy and Adam both participate in extracurricular activities.**
Ⓓ **Neither Timothy nor Adam participates in extracurricular activities.**

Question Number: 3

If you compare and contrast Timothy and Stanley, which statement is correct?

Ⓐ **Stanley participates in many extracurricular activities such as sports and chorus, but Timothy does not.**
Ⓑ **Stanley and Timothy both participate in extracurricular activities such as sports and chorus.**
Ⓒ **Neither Stanley nor Timothy participates in extracurricular activities.**
Ⓓ **Stanley enjoys solitary activities such as drawing, but Timothy enjoys group activities such as chorus and sports.**

Adam lives with his dad and his older brother Stanley. Adam and Stanley share a room. Most of the time Adam enjoys sharing a room with his brother, but there are times that he wished he had his own room. Being brothers, they have a lot in common; however, they are different in many ways.

Adam likes to spend time with his friends. If he is not with them, he is texting them or playing games with them online. Adam is always busy. He cannot stand to sit around and do nothing. In fact, the only time he is still is when he is sleeping. Adam plays football, basketball, soccer, and baseball. He loves to be involved in whatever is going on at school or at the town's youth center. He spends a lot of his time encouraging people to recycle and even volunteers at the youth center. Although he loves spending time with his friends, he is willing to give up time with them to help others.

Stanley loves to stay at home. He enjoys activities that can be done alone such as reading, drawing, and spending time with his dogs. Most days after school you can find him at home enjoying one of his favorite activities. He also thinks recycling is important and makes sure his family does it. Although he likes being alone, he enjoys volunteering at the youth center with his brother. He thinks it is important to make a difference in the lives others, which is why he thinks he would like to be a doctor. Adam and Stanley may be different in many ways, but they join together and make a difference in their community.

Question Number: 4

Compare and contrast Adam and his brother Stanley. Which statement is true?

Ⓐ **Both Adam and Stanley believe in recycling.**
Ⓑ **Neither Adam nor Stanley believes in recycling.**
Ⓒ **Adam believes in recycling, but Stanley does not.**
Ⓓ **Adam does not believe in recycling, but Stanley does.**

This year Jim and I had the most wonderful vacation compared to the one we took last year. This year Jim and I went to Hawaii, which is a much better place to visit than a hunting lodge in Alaska. The hotel we stayed in was a luxury suite. It included a big screen TV with all of the movie channels, a hot tub on the balcony, a small kitchen stocked with local fruits and vegetables, and a huge bed shaped like a pineapple. The weather in Hawaii could not have been any better. We enjoyed many hours on the beach sunbathing and playing volleyball. When we were not on the beach, we were in the ocean swimming or riding the waves on a surf board. Each night we enjoyed eating and dancing with all of our friends at a luau. Our week in Hawaii rushed by, making us wish we had planned a two-week vacation.

On the other hand, the hunting lodge we stayed in Alaska had no TV, a shower with barely warm water, a small cooler for our food, and cots to sleep on each night. The room wasn't even the worst part of the vacation. The weather was terrible. It rained the entire time we were there. Even with the rain, our guide expected us to go on the all-day fishing trip that was part of our vacation package. All we caught on that fishing trip was a cold from the rain. After the third day, we decided to cut our trip short and head for home. Without a doubt, we will be going back to Hawaii next year on our vacation.

Question Number: 5

Compare and contrast the Alaskan and Hawaiian vacations. Which statement is correct?

Ⓐ **Both had beautiful hotel rooms with nice accommodations.**
Ⓑ **The weather in Alaska was beautiful, but it rained the entire time they were in Hawaii.**
Ⓒ **The Hawaiian vacation was much more enjoyable than the Alaskan vacation.**
Ⓓ **The Alaskan vacation was much more enjoyable than the Hawaiian vacation.**

Lindsay, Scarlet, and Austin loved their aunts and were really excited. They ran upstairs and started getting their things together to take with them. They put everything in one bag that they would have to take to school with them. They were going to stay with Aunt Margaret for two nights and the last night with their Auntie Josephine.

At the end of the school day, the children came running out of classroom doors from all different directions. Aunt Margaret was waiting for her nieces and nephew at the entrance to the school. She was wearing a bright red suit with a sparkly cat pin on it. She also had on a proper wool hat to match. She noticed a scuff on her shoes when her nieces and nephew ran up to her.

She cried, "Oh, my goodness! I am so happy you are here. The children at your school are just a bunch of hooligans. I was nearly trampled while I was standing here! Let's go get in the car." Aunt Margaret pointed to a large, green four-door station wagon parked in the lot.

The next day, a funny-sounding honk came from the front of the house. The children ran outside and saw Auntie Jo sitting in her convertible. She was wearing a big cowboy hat. She wore a pair of polka dot shorts with a too large shirt.

Question Number: 6

Compare and contrast the way the two different aunts dressed.

Ⓐ **Auntie Jo and Aunt Margaret dressed the same.**
Ⓑ **Auntie Jo dressed very casually while Aunt Margaret dressed very properly.**
Ⓒ **Auntie Jo was wearing a skirt and Aunt Margaret was wearing a dress.**
Ⓓ **None of the above**

Question Number: 7

Compare and contrast the cars that the aunts drove.

Ⓐ **Auntie Jo had a fun convertible, and Aunt Margaret had a station wagon.**
Ⓑ **The two aunts had the same car.**
Ⓒ **Auntie Jo had a sedan, and Aunt Margaret had a convertible.**
Ⓓ **Neither of them had a car.**

The red tail hawks noticed something was happening to all the other animals living in Running Brook during the spring. The birds seemed to be losing their feathers. The bears were losing their fur. Mountain goats were complaining that their feet hurt. The beavers had cavities, and the deer all seemed to be catching colds. The red squirrels had gotten so fat they almost could not make it across the road.

Hawk made an observation. He was pretty sure that everything started happening when the town's first fast food restaurant opened. Forest Fawn thought he brought a great idea to the town and that he could make some extra money by opening a place to eat something quickly. Forest Fawn knew how difficult it was to find food during winter months. He thought he was doing his friends a favor.

The restaurant sold birdseed in five different flavors. For the bears, Forest Fawn sold artificially flavored honey and salmon cakes and deep-fried berries. Salted tree moss with lichen-flavored chips was on the shelf for the mountain goats and deer.

Question Number: 8

What was happening to the animals once the fast food restaurant opened?

Ⓐ **Birds were losing their feathers, and bears were losing patches of fur.**
Ⓑ **Beavers got cavities, and deer had colds.**
Ⓒ **Bad things were happening to the animals because of the food they were eating.**
Ⓓ **The squirrels were getting fat and the mountain goats complained about their feet.**

Question Number: 9

Compare what happened to the beavers and the birds.

Ⓐ **The birds lost their feathers, and the beavers had cavities.**
Ⓑ **Tthe birds had colds, and the beavers lost their fur.**
Ⓒ **The birds liked the candy, and the beavers liked the syrup**
Ⓓ **The birds had sore feet and the beavers gained weight.**

Beatrice was so excited. This was truly a special day for her. She looked down and saw that her cup was sparkling with clean and cold water. She couldn't believe it was real as she had never seen water like that before. She slowly took a sip and it tasted so fresh. Her mother always told her how important water is.

The only way that Beatrice was able to get her water in the past was from the dirty water in a ditch not far from her home. Otherwise, they would have to walk for miles to reach other areas that had water. The water wasn't very clean in the other areas, either. In fact, most of the time, this water had a horrible smell and was brownish in color. Beatrice and her family knew it wasn't great but they didn't have any choice. The water that they drank was contaminated, making Beatrice feel sick often.

The water they mostly use is from streams, rivers, and lakes and is used for cooking, taking baths, and washing clothes. This water is contaminated from chemicals in the products they use and can cause diseases, such as typhus, cholera, dysentery, and malaria.

Question Number: 10

How did Beatrice get her water in the past compared to how she gets her water now?

- Ⓐ **They have always gotten their water from a faucet in their kitchen.**
- Ⓑ **They used to get it from the well and now they'll get it from the faucet.**
- Ⓒ **They used to get it from the dirty stream, and now they will have a well in the village.**
- Ⓓ **None of the above**

End of Reading: Literature

Answer Key and Detailed Explanations

Reading: Literature
Finding Detail in the Story (RL.4.1)

Question No.	Answer	Detailed Explanation
1	B	The second choice is correct. When Mary began reading her story to her class, those are the first words she read. The title of a story goes at the top of the page, and those are the first words read when sharing a story aloud.
2	C	The third choice is correct. The passage states that "However, there was one part about every Friday at school that Mary did not enjoy, and that was when she had to share her story in front of the class."
3	C	The third choice is correct, because the passage stated that, "The teacher made all the children share on Friday afternoons."
4	A	Ellie's father explains that her wings help her gather speed and go fast. Although option B is a fact from the story, it does not show how Ellie can run faster, but how she can stop fast.
5	B	The second choice is correct, because the passage states that "You can also use them as brakes while turning and stopping." You refers to Ellie and other ostriches, and them refers to their wings.
6	D	According to the story, Alexander realized "that the horse was terrified of its own shadow, and he turned the horse towards the sun so that its shadow fell behind it. This calmed the horse, and the prince proudly rode away."
7	C	Choice C is correct, because cups and ornaments are objects that are useful to people. The first two choices are details describing the ostrich's size and weight.
8	D	The fourth choice is correct. It referred to the vacation as a "nightmare," and told that they "cut their trip short." If they were enjoying their trip, they would have stayed the whole time as planned instead of leaving early.
9	A	The first answer choice is correct. Because the author wished the vacation could have been two weeks instead of one shows that the vacation was wonderful.
10	B	Their favorite vacation spot was Hawaii and option B describes the hotel in Hawaii. Options C and D are statements that describe the Hawaii vacation but they do not describe the hotel.

Inferring (RL.4.1)

Question No.	Answer	Detailed Explanation
1	C	The third choice is correct. We know that the poet was suprised to hear a song from the shell, because the poet "listened hard, / And it was really true." When a person is surprised by something or can't believe it, it makes sense that they would gather more information before confirming that it is true.
2	C	The third choice is correct. We know the horse was scared, because the passage said "Realizing that the horse was terrified of its own shadow." Terrified means the same thing as scared.
3	D	The fourth choice is correct. We can infer that Cindy did not like what her mother had cooked, because she asked if she could cook something else (the frozen pizza).
4	B	The second choice is correct. We can infer that Mary began reading her story in front of the class, because the last sentence said that she got out of her seat and walked to the front of the room after her name was called. We know that was the signal to start reading the story.
5	C	The third choice is correct. The passage tells us that Mary really enjoys writing stories. We know that many parents support their children at things they are good at.
6	C	The third choice is correct. We can infer that Ben and his dad were going to a local mountain, because the passage says that there was a new blanket of snow outside. Also, his dad told him to grab his skiis. Our background knowledge tells us that people ski on snow-covered mountains.
7	C	The third choice is correct. We can infer that this takes place in the early morning at sunrise, because the sky was turning from dark to pinkish-yellow. We know that at nighttime, the sky is dark. We also know that it becomes light in the early morning.
8	D	The fourth choice is correct. The author says she, "lay on the windowsill." These are things only a cat would do. The mention of birds in the 5th sentence is also a clue, because cats prey on birds.
9	A	The first choice is correct. We can infer that it is summer, because the passage tells us that it is hot. We know that people go surfing in the summertime because the hot weather makes the ocean just right for swimming and surfing.

Question No.	Answer	Detailed Explanation
10	A	The second choice is correct. We can infer that Susie's family lives near the beach, because the passage says that they drove there in a car. If they did not live near the beach, they would have to travel for several hours or fly on an airplane to get to the beach. The passage did not imply that they would be traveling a long distance.

Finding the Theme (RL.4.2)

Question No.	Answer	Detailed Explanation
1	C	The third choice is correct. Fred spent a lot of time worrying about visiting the dentist and got himself really worked up. When he actually visited the dentist, nothing bad happened to him. He realized that he was wrong for worrying.
2	B	The second choice is correct. Opal felt really bad when she acted dishonestly. After she told the truth, she instantly felt better.
3	A	The first choice is correct. The quilt did not cost much money, but it had a lot of sentimental value to Libby.
4	B	The second choice is correct. In this story, a homemade gift (the quilt) was better than an expensive one, but that is a detail and not the theme.
5	C	The third choice is correct. Rhonda's new school is different than her old one, but Rhonda liked the different things at her new school.
6	D	The fourth choice is correct. Telling her little brother that she was sorry didn't make Polly's little brother feel better. Polly's little brother started to feel better when Polly read him a story.
7	C	The third choice is correct. Since Karen worked hard and completed her assignments on time, she received an A in the class.
8	A	The first choice is correct. If Mr. Toad had shared his food, he wouldn't have been so full and would have been able to escape the hunter.
9	C	The third choice is correct. Frank's friends quit asking him to hang out, because all he wanted to do was quote information from books.
10	C	The third choice is correct. If the monkey wasn't greedy and just let go of the cookies, his hand wouldn't be stuck in the cookie jar.

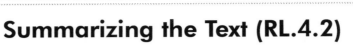

Summarizing the Text (RL.4.2)

Question No.	Answer	Detailed Explanation
1	B	The second choice is correct, because it tells only the important information from the passage.
2	A	The first choice is correct, because it tells only the most important information from the passage.
3	A	The first choice is correct, because it gives only the most important information from the passage. Some of the information in the other answer choices is out of order.
4	A	The first choice is correct, because it tells the most important information in the passage.
5	B	The second choice is correct, because it tells the most important information in the passage.
6	C	The third choice is correct, because it tells the most important details from the passage.
7	C	The third choice is correct, because it has nothing to do with the main idea of the passage. The passage is about Mary being good at creative writing, but being afraid to share her stories in front of her class. The third choice is correct, because it wasn't even from the passage.
8	A	The first choice is correct, because it tells the main idea and the most important information from the story.
9	C	The third choice is correct, because it gives the main idea of the passage and the most important details.
10	A	The first choice is correct. The first choice is not an important piece of information from the story.

Describing Characters (RL.4.3)

1	C	The third choice is correct. We know that Timothy is responsible, because the passage said that he gets up every day to perform his dog walking job. We know that Timothy is ambitious, because Timothy believes he can continue his dog walking job and participate in extracurricular activities at the same time.
2	B	The second answer is correct. We know that Timothy wouldn't help someone cheat on a test, because the passage said that "he is always honest and expects others to be honest."

Question No.	Answer	Detailed Explanation
3	B	The second choice is correct. We know that Fred was afraid and didn't understand why he had to go to the dentist, because the passage said that he had heard horror stories all of his life about the dentist and he thought the dentist would torture him. The passage also said that he didn't understand why his mom thought he needed to go since none of his teeth were hurting.
4	C	The third choice is correct. We know that Fred felt relieved after his visit to the dentist, because he said the chair was comfortable and the dentist was nice. The last sentence of the passage said that it wasn't as bad as he thought it would be.
5	A	The first choice is correct. Stanley is solitary, because he likes to spend his time doing things by himself. Stanley is caring, because he volunteers at the recycling center.
6	A	The first choice is correct. We know that Adam and Stanley like and respect each other, because they enjoy volunteering together at the recycling center.
7	B	The second choice is correct. We know that Adam is thoughtful, because he volunteers his time at a recycling center. We know that Adam is outgoing, because he likes to spend all of his time with his friends.
8	A	The first choice is correct. We know that Beau was anxious, because he was in a situation where most kids would be anxious. The passage also told us that he was fidgeting and playing with his button.
9	A	The first choice is correct. Libby's grandmother was nervous, because she was afraid that Libby would not like the quilt.
10	D	The fourth choice is correct. Libby's grandmother was happy after Libby opened up the quilt, because Libby loved the present.

Describing the Setting (RL.4.3)

Question No.	Answer	Detailed Explanation
1	A	The first choice is correct. The first sentence of the passage tells us that the story takes place two thousand five hundred years ago.
2	B	The second choice is correct. The setting for the second paragraph is an automobile, because it tells us that Fred and his mother were on their way to the dentist. People usually take automobiles to the dentist.
3	C	The third choice is correct. Huckleberry Hound was on the porch at the beginning of the story. The first sentence of the passage tells us so.
4	B	The second choice is correct. Huckleberry Hound chased the rabbit in the field. The second sentence of the passage tells us so.
5	A	The first choice is correct. Huckleberry Hound was in the yard at the end of the story. The last sentence of the passage tells us so.
6	B	The second choice is correct. The writer was at school. The second sentence of the passage tells us so.
7	A	The first choice is correct. The writer dropped her ice cream at the ice cream shop. The last sentence of the passage tells us so.
8	C	The third choice is correct. The third paragraph says "at the end of the school day."
9	C	The third choice is correct. The story takes place in her classroom at Mary's school. The whole passage is about one of Mary's classes.
10	B	The second choice is correct. The story takes place her classroom outside in a yard. The first sentence of the passage tells us so.

Describing Events (RL.4.3)

1	C	The third choice is correct. We know Timmy is saving up for youth camp, because the last sentence of the passage tells us so.
2	B	The second choice is correct. We know that Timmy gets up at 5 a.m. to walk dogs, because the third sentence of the second paragraph tells us so.

Question No.	Answer	Detailed Explanation
3	C	The third choice is correct. We know that Fred is worried about going to the dentist because people who are scared often tremble in fear.
4	B	The second choice is correct. We know that Fred thinks the dentist will put him in a chair and use a huge drill on him, because that is what the second paragraph of the passage is about.
5	A	The first choice is correct. The last paragraph of the passage tells us that the dentist showed Fred how to brush and floss his teeth.
6	D	The fourth choice is correct. The last paragraph of the passage tells us that Adam and Stanley enjoy volunteering at the youth center together.
7	C	The third choice is correct. Sharing her story in front of the class made Mary nervous. The third paragraph in the passage tells us this.
8	D	The fourth choice is correct. The kids were excited about being dismissed from school, and Aunt Margaret happened to be in the way. A scuff is only a very small mark.
9	C	The third choice is correct. The parents are going out of town. The first sentence of the passage tells us this.
10	C	The passages show that Mary was very shy and Timmy was not. Although option A is a correct statement, it does not describe how they felt about presenting.

Figurative Language(RL.4.4)

1	D	"Twinkled like diamonds" is a simile. A simile compares two things using like or as. The way the girl's eyes twinkle is being compared to how diamonds twinkle.
2	B	This is a metaphor. A metaphor is a direct comparison of 2 unlike objects. Her heart is being compared to stone. Stone is hard, and her heart was hard (meaning she was not very sensitive).
3	C	This is a metaphor. The sound the bird made was being compared to music, meaning it made a pleasant, entertaining sound.
4	D	Birds eat very little, and Suzy eats very little.
5	B	A compass guides people in the right location. The man's wife guides him to the right paths in life.

Question No.	Answer	Detailed Explanation
6	D	A lemon is sour and unpleasant. A car that doesn't run well is unpleasant.
7	D	A simile compares two objects using like or as. This simile compares the hardness of the biscuits to the hardness of rocks.
8	C	Angels are kind. Janice is kind.
9	C	Oxen are strong. Jimmy is strong.
10	B	A metaphor directly compares 2 unlike objects. Libby is being compared to a road hog.

Text Structure (RL.4.5)

1	D	The Three Little Pigs is told in sequence or chronological order. That means that the events are told in the order that they happened.
2	D	Descriptive texts tell the characteristics of a particular subject.
3	D	This is a narrative text, because the writer is describing an event in his or her life.
4	C	Sequencing and Chronological texts tell about events in the order that they happened.
5	D	Sequencing and Chronological Order texts tell the events in the order that they happened.
6	D	Problem/Solution texts start out explaining a problem. Then, they offer a solution. The problem in this passage is that Beau wanted a dog. The solution was for him to keep his room clean.
7	A	When an author adds descriptions about characters' emotions and feelings, it allows the reader to connect more deeply with the characters.
8	C	Text about a particular topic in no specific order.
9	B	This is a compare and contrast passage, because it tells the similarities and differences of two different subjects.
10	C	Problem and solution texts describe a problem, then they explain a solution to the problem. Germs are a problem, and the passage explains how to deal with them.

Point of View (RL.4.6)

Question No.	Answer	Detailed Explanation
1	B	Second person point of view is when the writer is talking directly to the reader.
2	A	First person point of view is when one of the characters is telling the story. Pronouns such as I and me are used.
3	C	Third person point of view is when the story is told by someone who is not a character in the story.
4	B	Second person point of view is when the writer is speaking directly to the reader.
5	C	Third person point of view is when the story is being told by someone who is not a character in the story.
6	A	First person point of view is when one of the characters in the story is telling it. Pronouns such as I and me are used.
7	A	First person point of view is when one of the characters in the story is telling the story. Pronouns such as I and me are used.
8	A	First person point of view is when the story is being told by one of the characters in the story. Pronouns such as I and me are used.
9	C	Third person point of view is when the story is told by a someone who is not a character in the story.
10	C	Third person point of view is when the story is being told by a person who is not a character in the story.

Visual Connections (RL.4.7)

1	B	The picture of the female in front of a chalkboard is appropriate, because this story takes place in a school classroom and Mary is speaking to her class.
2	C	The third choice is correct, because it is about baby monkeys. There are baby monkeys in the picture.
3	C	The third choice is correct, because it is about a kitten at a construction site. The kitten in the picture is in a concrete pipe.
4	C	The third choice is correct, because it is about singing. The girl in the picture is holding a microphone and singing.
5	D	The fourth choice is correct, because it is about a sandcastle shaped like a dragon.

Question No.	Answer	Detailed Explanation
6	B	The passage is about a way that a teacher helps a student learn to read. A photo of a teacher and a student with a book would be appropriate.
7	D	Although each description of images could be found in the story, only option D describes the moral of the story. When the friend walks away without giving advice, the man reminds him he made need advice someday too.
8	C	The illustration is from the book <u>Treasure Island</u> where the young boy is saying goodbye to his mother. The hug and the look on the boy's face help the reader determine this is a goodbye hug filled with much longing.
9	A	A Venn Diagram allows the reader to list out character-istics or details of the story to determine if there are any overlapping ideas. In the case of these two passages, both students clearly loved writing, even if they had different approaches to sharing their story. Because we did not read the stories, we do not know if they were fiction.
10	B	Option B is the closest image to what Timmy could show to add depth to his story. The reader does not know much about his story other than it involves a spaceship. It does not mention an elephant; that is Mary's story. It does not mention a boy playing soccer. Option D shows a student who is raising his hand, possibly in excitement like Timmy; however, that does not add depth to his story, just the paragraph describing his day.

Comparing and Contrasting (RL.4.9)

1	C	The third choice is correct, because it tells how Fred felt afraid at first but relieved at the end.
2	C	The third choice is correct, because it tells a way that the two boys are alike. Comparing means telling how one or more subjects are alike.
3	D	To contrast means to tell how two subjects are different. The fourth choice tells what Stanley likes to do and what Timothy likes to do.
4	A	The first choice is correct. Both boys volunteer at the recy-cling center.
5	C	The third choice is correct, because it tells how the people favored the Hawaiian vacation over the Alaskan vacation.

Question No.	Answer	Detailed Explanation
6	B	The second choice is correct, because it tells how each aunt dresses.
7	A	The first choice is correct, because it tells what kind of car each aunt drives.
8	C	The third choice is correct, because it tells what happened to the animals after the restaurant opened. The different animals all had various complaints.
9	A	The first choice is correct, because it told what happened to the birds and to the beavers.
10	C	The third choice is correct, because it correctly tells where they used to get their water and where they get their water now.

Notes

Reading: Informational Text

It's All in the Details (RI.4.1)

The ostrich is the largest bird in the world, but it cannot fly. Its legs are so strong and long that it can travel faster by running. Ostriches use their wings to help them gather speed when they start to run. They also use them as brakes when turning and stopping.

Ostriches have been known to run at a rate of 60 miles an hour. This is faster than horses can run and as fast as most people drive cars.

These huge birds stand as tall as a horse and sometimes weigh as much as 298 pounds. In their home country of Africa, they are often seen with some of the larger animals. The zebra, which is also a fast runner, seems to be one of their favorite companions.

An ostrich egg weighs one pound, which is as much as two dozen chicken eggs. Ostrich eggs are delicious and are often used for food by people in Africa. The shells are also made into cups and beautiful ornaments.

Question Number: 1

Why is it a good thing that the Ostrich can run, rather than fly?

Ⓐ **The Ostrich does not enjoy flying.**
Ⓑ **The Ostrich is able to fly.**
Ⓒ **The Ostrich is not able to fly.**
Ⓓ **The Ostrich can travel faster by running.**

Question Number: 2

Devon says that Ostriches are shy and solitary birds. Which detail in the text proves him wrong?

Ⓐ "Ostrich eggs are delicious and are often used for food by people in Africa."
Ⓑ "An Ostrich egg wieghs one pound."
Ⓒ "These huge birds stand as tall as a horse..."
Ⓓ "The zebra, which is also a fast runner, seems to be one of their favorite companions."

The blue whale is quite an extraordinary creature. To begin with, it is a mammal that lives its entire life in the ocean. The size of its body is amazing. This whale can grow up to 98 feet long and weigh as much as 200 tons, making it the largest known animal to have ever existed. Its body is long and elegantly tapered, unlike other whales which have a rounder, stockier build. Their build, along with their extreme size, gives them a unique appearance and the ability to move more gracefully and at greater speeds than one might imagine. They can reach speeds up to 31 mph for short periods of time. Their normal traveling speed is around 12 mph, but they slow to 3.1 mph when feeding. Although they are extremely large animals, they eat small shrimp-like creatures called krill. Since the krill are so small, the blue whale eats about four tons daily as they swim deep in the ocean.

Unlike other whales that live in small, close-knit groups called pods, blue whales live and travel alone or with one other whale. While traveling through the ocean, they surface to breathe air into their lungs through blowholes. They emerge from the ocean, spewing water out of their blowhole, roll, and reenter the water with a grand splash of their large tail. They make loud, deep, and rumbling low-frequency sounds that travel great distances, which allow them to communicate with other whales as far as 100 miles away. Their cries can be felt as much as heard. Their resonating call makes them the loudest animal on Earth. If you ever have the opportunity to see or hear a blue whale, it will be an experience you will not soon forget.

Question Number: 3

Angel argues that the blue whale is a solitary creature. What evidence from the text best supports his point?

Ⓐ "Unlike other whales that live in small, close-knit groups called pods, blue whales live and travel alone or with one other whale."
Ⓑ "This whale can grow up to 98 feet long and weigh as much as 200 tons, making it the largest known animal to have ever existed."
Ⓒ "Although they are extremely large animals, they eat small shrimp-like creatures called krill."
Ⓓ None of the above

If you join our music club, you will receive 4 free CDs. These CDs are yours to keep, whether or not you decide to cancel your membership. If you decide to remain a member and purchase just 2 CDs at regular price, you will get to choose another 3 free CDs. After your first purchase at regular price, you will receive 10 points for every CD purchased thereafter. For each 30 points you collect, you get to choose another free CD! If you want to earn even more free CDs, then have your friends join, too. For each friend who joins using your name, you will receive 3 more free CDs. The best part is that you get 3 free CDs every time you have another friend join our club, so join today and start collecting your favorite CDs.

Question Number: 4

What detail from the text encourages music club members to get their friends to join the club?

Ⓐ "If you join our music club, you will receive 4 free CDs."
Ⓑ "After your first purchase at regular price, you will receive 10 points for every CD purchased thereafter."
Ⓒ "If you want to earn even more free CDs, then have your friends join, too."
Ⓓ "The best part is that you get 3 free CDs every time you have another friend join our club…"

Have you ever wondered what happened to the dinosaurs that once roamed the Earth? Well, scientists have developed several theories throughout the years. One such theory is that a gigantic meteorite crashed into our planet, causing a massive dust cloud to cover the Earth. The dust cloud was so enormous that it blocked the rays of the Sun from reaching Earth. This caused all of the plants to die, which led to the herbivores dying. Subsequently, the large carnivores also died, leaving the planet with no dinosaurs.

Question Number: 5

Amelia asserts that dinosaurs definitely died because a giant meteorite crashed into Earth. What key words from the text would help Terrance to make a counter point?

Ⓐ "One such theory…"
Ⓑ "…a giant meteorite crashed into our planet"
Ⓒ "…leaving the planet with no dinosaurs."
Ⓓ All of the above

Do you like frogs? Do you know what a spring peeper is?

Spring peepers are tiny little tree frogs that live in wooded areas near ponds. Although these little frogs are tiny, only about an inch big, they make a very loud sound. They are found mostly in the central and eastern parts of the United States. So, when the weather begins to get warmer after winter, these little frogs start to sing. Their "peep," which is why they are called spring peepers, can be heard for miles around. They live near ponds so they can lay their eggs in the water.

When the weather starts getting colder again, the spring peepers start to go into hiding. They hibernate under logs or any other place they can find in the forest to protect them from the cold. For example, sometimes they hide under fallen leaves or even in a small hole in the ground.

Question Number: 6

Which paragraph contains details that support Monique's idea that people are most likely to see spring peepers during warm weather months?

Ⓐ **Paragraph 1**
Ⓑ **Paragraph 2**
Ⓒ **Paragraph 3**
Ⓓ **Paragraphs 2 and 3**

Most people refer to koalas as koala bears, but they are not bears at all. They are actually marsupials and are in the same family as the wombat. Koalas live in eucalyptus forests in eastern and southeastern Australia. Adult koalas are one of only three mammals that can survive on a diet of eucalyptus leaves. These leaves contain 50% water, requiring them to seldom drink water since they obtain it through the leaves.

Since the koala is a marsupial, the baby crawls into the mother's pouch as soon as it is born. Baby koalas are called "joeys." When they are born, they are blind, hairless, and less than one inch long. They remain in their mother's pouch for the next six months, feeding first on the mother's milk and then on a substance called "pap" in addition to the mother's milk. Joeys continue to take their mother's milk until they are a year old. The young koala will remain with its mother until the appearance of another joey in the mother's pouch.

Question Number: 7

What detail in the text explains why someone is not likely to see a koala in northwestern Australia?

Ⓐ **"Koalas live in eucalyptus forests..."**
Ⓑ **"They are marsupials and are in the same family as the wombat."**
Ⓒ **"Koalas live...in eastern and southeastern Australia."**
Ⓓ **"When they are born, they are blind, hairless, and less than one inch long."**

There are four types of tissues that are formed as cells join together and function as a group. Each type of tissue has a distinctive structure and does a specific job. Muscle tissue is made up of long, narrow muscle cells. Muscle tissue makes your body parts move by contracting and relaxing. Connective tissue is what holds up your body and connects its parts together. Bone is made up of connective tissue. Nerve tissue is made up of long nerve cells that branch through your body and carry messages throughout the body. Epithelial tissue is made of wide, flat epithelial cells. This tissue lines the surfaces inside the body and forms the outer layer of the skin. Groups of tissue join together to form the organs in our body such as the heart, liver, lungs, brain, and kidneys just to name a few. Subsequently these organs work together to form our body systems. Each system works in complete coordination with one another, as well as with the other systems of the body.

Question Number: 8

What job does muscle tissue perform in the body?

Ⓐ **It holds up your body.**
Ⓑ **It allows your body to move**
Ⓒ **It allows messages to travel through your body.**
Ⓓ **It forms the outer layer of skin.**

Question Number: 9

What job does the epithelial tissue perform?

Ⓐ **It holds up your body.**
Ⓑ **It allows your body to move.**
Ⓒ **It allows messages to travel through your body.**
Ⓓ **It forms the outer layer of skin.**

2362 West Main Street
Jojo, TX 98456

June 16, 2010

Dear Mr. Seymour:

I ordered a Magic Racing Top from your Company. The toy was delivered to me today in a package that was badly damaged. I took a picture of the box before I opened it, which I am sending to you as proof of damage. The toy inside was broken due, I'm sure, to the damage to the package during shipping.

This toy was to be a gift for my friend's birthday. There is not enough time before his party to wait on a replacement toy; therefore, I no longer need the toy. I would like for you to refund my money. If you would like for me to return the broken toy, please send a prepaid shipping label.

Thank you for handling this matter for me. I look forward to hearing from you and hope we can satisfactorily resolve this problem.

Sincerely,
Tim West

Question Number: 10

Dominique argues that the writer of this letter was pleased with the toy company be cause he says, "please," and "if you would like." Does this evidence do a good job of supporting her argument?

Ⓐ Yes. These are very polite words, so he is clearly pleased with the toy company.

Ⓑ Yes. He also says, "Thank you for handling this matter for me."

Ⓒ No. He is being polite, but he also says the package he ordered was, "badly damaged," and, "I would like for you to refund my money."

Ⓓ No. He wants to satisfactorily resolve the problem.

The Main Idea (RI.4.2)

The ostrich is the largest bird in the world, but it cannot fly. Its legs are so strong and long that it can travel faster by running. Ostriches use their wings to help them gather speed when they start to run. They also use them as brakes when turning and stopping.

Ostriches have been known to run at a rate of 60 miles an hour. This is faster than horses can run and as fast as most people drive cars.

These huge birds stand as tall as a horse and sometimes weigh as much as 298pounds. In their home country of Africa, they are often seen with some of the larger animals. The zebra, which is also a fast runner, seems to be one of their favorite companions.

An ostrich egg weighs one pound, which is as much as two dozen chicken eggs. Ostrich eggs are delicious and are often used for food by people in Africa. The shells are also made into cups and beautiful ornaments.

Question Number: 1

What is the main idea of the passage?

Ⓐ Ostriches are great because their eggs are delicious,
Ⓑ The ostrich is the largest bird with many interesting characteristics.
Ⓒ The ostrich is the largest bird but it cannot fly.
Ⓓ The ostrich lives in Africa.

Question Number: 2

Which details support the main idea of the passage?

Ⓐ Ostriches are great because their eggs are delicious,
Ⓑ The ostrich is the smallest bird and can run very fast.
Ⓒ The ostrich is the largest bird that can fly very fast.
Ⓓ The ostrich lives in Africa.

Did you know that the coconut tree is very useful to people? Each and every part of the tree can be used for a variety of things. For example, the coconut fruit, which we get from the tree, is very nutritious and is used in cooking many different kinds of food. Coconut milk, which is extracted from the coconut, tastes very delicious and is used to prepare a variety of sweet dishes.

Oil can be extracted from a dried coconut. Coconut oil is a very good moisturizer. It is used in many beauty products like body wash, face wash, shampoos and conditioners. The oil is also used for cooking some of the tropical foods. Some coconut trees grow straight and tall, and some trees are very short. Coconut trees do not have branches. They have long leaves which grow right at the top of the tree. The leaves are used for many different things. Leaf ribs are made into brooms, and fiber is obtained from the outer cover of the nut and used for mattresses, rugs, etc. The trunk is used to make logs for small boats. It is also used for firewood. The sweet water of the tender coconut quenches the thirst during the hot summer months and is also very healthy.

Question Number: 3

What is the most appropriate title for this passage?

Ⓐ **The Coconut Tree & Its Uses**
Ⓑ **The Coconut Tree**
Ⓒ **Things We Get from the Coconut**
Ⓓ **Tall Coconut Trees**

Alex the Great

Nearly two thousand five hundred years ago, there lived a king called Alexander the Great. He was the son of Philip II of Macedonia. When Alexander was a boy, a magnificent horse for sale was brought to the court of his father. The animal was to be sold for thirteen talents. Talents are ancient coins. Many were eager to buy the horse but none could get close enough to saddle the restless animal. He was wild and it was not possible to ride him.

Alexander pleaded with his father to let him try. Realizing that the horse was terrified of its own shadow, he turned the horse towards the sun so that its shadow fell behind it. This calmed the

horse and the prince proudly rode away. Observing this, his father said, "My son, look for a king-dom worthy of your greatness. Macedonia is too small for you."

That is exactly what Alexander tried to do when he grew up. He fought many battles and always rode Bucephalus. (That was the horse's name.) Friendship and trust grew between man and horse. When Bucephalus died of wounds received in battle, Alexander was heartbroken and deeply mourned the loss of his horse. He wished that he had died along with it.

Question Number: 4

What is the main idea of this passage?

Ⓐ **Alexander's love for animals**
Ⓑ **Alexander's smartness and greatness**
Ⓒ **Taming a wild horse**
Ⓓ **King Philip II**

Environmental pollution causes the poisoning of our immediate surroundings. It hurts Mother Earth by disturbing nature's balance, which is very important for the survival of all living beings. Today's environmental problems arise from four distinct forms of pollution that affect the soil, water, air and sound levels. Dumping massive amounts of industrial wastes and household refuse causes land pollution. Pesticides and fertilizers used in agriculture also pollute the soil. Plastics are also major pollutants.

Overgrazing and deforestation lead to the formation of deserts and wastelands. Deserts already cover 40 percent of the Earth's surface.

The presence of harmful wastes in water makes it unclean for human and animal use. Even aquatic life suffers due to thousands of tons of oil that get spilled into the seas and oceans. The air that we breathe is contaminated by smoke and dust in the atmosphere. Lung diseases are common when the air is polluted. Noise pollution in cities has grown beyond human tolerance. Pollution is also responsible for global warming or heating up of the environment. Thus pollution is becoming a serious problem for the whole world.

Question Number: 5

Which detail in the above passage tells us that the soil is being polluted?

Ⓐ **The oil spills in the seas and oceans.**
Ⓑ **Smoke and dust in the air**
Ⓒ **Dumping of industrial wastes and household refuse**
Ⓓ **Global warming**

Beautiful seashells that are washed ashore on beaches by ocean waves have always fascinated human beings. Shells come in a wonderful array of shapes, sizes, and colors. Shells are actually made by marine creatures to serve as their homes. Seashells are, quite simply, skeletons of mollusks. Mollusks are a class of water animals that have soft bodies and hard outer coverings, called shells. Human beings carry their bony skeletons inside and wear their soft bodies on the outside. But mollusks do just the opposite.

Shells are very durable and outlive the soft-bodied animals that produce them. Shells may be univalve or bivalve. Univalve shells are made up of just one unit, whereas bivalve shells have two units or two halves. Snails have univalve shells and oysters have bivalve shells. Shells protect the soft-bodied animals from rough surfaces that can harm their bodies and from predators.

Question Number: 6

The main role of a seashell is:

Ⓐ **To look beautiful**
Ⓑ **To serve as a home for mollusks**
Ⓒ **To float to the shores**
Ⓓ **To be collected by divers**

Sacagawea is a famous Native American from the Shoshone tribe. She became known because she helped two men, explorers named Lewis and Clark, find their way through the unexplored west. Before she was able to do that, however, she was kidnapped when she was 12 years old by an enemy Native American tribe called the Hidatsa. Then, legend has it, the chief of the Hidatsa tribe sold Sacagawea into slavery.

In 1804, she became an interpreter and guide for a group of explorers led by Lewis and Clark and she helped them find their way from near the Dakotas to the Pacific Ocean. She became a famous Native American in our history for being brave and helping these men discover unknown territory.

Question Number: 7

What would be a good title for the above story?

Ⓐ **Sacagawea: A Shoshone Woman**
Ⓑ **Sacagawea: An Amazing Woman**
Ⓒ **Sacagawea: Kidnapped by the Hidatsa**
Ⓓ **Sacagawea: Sold to a Fur Trader**

Question Number: 8

What is the main idea of the story above?

Ⓐ   Sacagawea was a woman who did so many things that women didn't do at the time and she will be remembered as part of American history.

Ⓑ   Sacagawea's life was amazing.

Ⓒ   Sacagawea helped two men explore the west.

Ⓓ   What Sacagawea did will be remembered forever.

Bischon frise is a very different breed of dog. They have white fluffy hair and tiny, black eyes. Years ago, this funny little breed was used as circus dogs. Many people keep them as pets, because they are hypoallergenic. This means that people with allergies aren't allergic to them. They don't shed, so they won't leave hair all over your house.

Question Number: 9

What is the main idea of the passage?

Ⓐ   Bichon frise is a unique breed of dogs.

Ⓑ   Bichon frise used to be circus dogs.

Ⓒ   Bichon frise are hypoallergenic.

Ⓓ   Bichon frise have white hair and black eyes.

Have you ever wondered what happened to the dinosaurs that once roamed the Earth? Well, scientists have developed several theories throughout the years. One such theory is that a gigantic meteorite crashed into our planet, causing a massive dust cloud to cover the Earth. The dust cloud was so enormous that it blocked the rays of the Sun from reaching Earth. This caused all of the plants to die, which lead to the herbivores to die off. Subsequently, the large carnivores also died, leaving the planet with no dinosaurs.

Question Number: 10

Which detail supports the idea that scientists believe a meteorite crashed into the planet and killed off the dinosaurs?

Ⓐ   Scientists have developed several theories throughout the years.

Ⓑ   Scientists wondered what happened to the dinosaurs that once roamed the Earth.

Ⓒ   The dust cloud was so enormous that it blocked the rays of the Sun from reaching Earth.

Ⓓ   Leaving the planet with no dinosaurs.

Using Details to Explain the Text (RI.4.3)

Digestive System

The digestive system is made up of the esophagus, stomach, liver, gall bladder, pancreas, large and small intestines, appendix, and rectum. Digestion actually begins in the mouth when food is chewed and mixed with saliva. Muscles in the esophagus push food into the stomach where it mixes with digestive juices. While in the stomach, food is broken down into nutrients and turns into a thick liquid. The food then moves into the small intestines where more digestive juices complete the breaking down of the food. It is in the small intestines that nutrients are absorbed into the blood and carried throughout the body. The leftover material that is unusable by the body moves into the large intestines where the body absorbs the water that is contained in it before passing it from the body through the rectum.

Question Number: 1

What event begins the digestive process?

Ⓐ **The small intestine absorbing nutrients**
Ⓑ **Muscles in the esophagus pushing food into the stomach**
Ⓒ **Chewing food and allowing it to mix with saliva**
Ⓓ **The esophagus**

Question Number: 2

How do nutrients that are absorbed from food move though the body?

Ⓐ **They develop the ability to swim through the body's fluids in a tiny school bus.**
Ⓑ **The digestive juices in the small intestine break them down.**
Ⓒ **They move through the esophagus and into the stomach.**
Ⓓ **They are absorbed into the blood, which carries them to other parts of the body.**

The blue whale is quite an extraordinary creature. To begin with, it is a mammal that lives its entire life in the ocean. The size of its body is amazing. This whale can grow up to 98 feet long and weigh as much as 200 tons, making it the largest known animal to have ever existed. Its body is long and elegantly tapered, unlike other whales which have a rounder, stockier build. Their build, along with their extreme size, gives them a unique appearance and the ability to move more gracefully and at greater speeds than one might imagine. They can reach speeds up to 31 mph for short periods of time. Their normal traveling speed is around 12 mph, but they slow to 3.1 mph when feeding. Although they are extremely large animals, they eat small shrimp-like creatures called krill. Since the krill are so small, the blue whale eats about four tons daily as they swim deep in the ocean.

Unlike other whales that live in small, close-knit groups called pods, blue whales live and travel alone or with one other whale. While traveling through the ocean, they surface to breathe air into their lungs through blowholes. They emerge from the ocean, spewing water out of their blowhole, roll, and reenter the water with a grand splash of their large tail. They make loud, deep, and rumbling low frequency sounds that travel great distances, which allow them to communicate with

other whales as far as 100 miles away. Their cries can be felt as much as heard. Their resonating call makes them the loudest animal on Earth. If you ever have the opportunity to see or hear a blue whale, it will be an experience you will not soon forget.

Question Number: 3

How do blue whales breathe?

Ⓐ **They use their blowholes to process oxygen found at deep ocean depths.**
Ⓑ **They spew water out of their blowholes and then rise to the surface to breathe air.**
Ⓒ **They rise to the surface, spew water out of their blowholes, and then breathe air in through their blowholes.**
Ⓓ **None of the above**

Question Number: 4

How are blue whales able to communicate with other whales from great distances away?

Ⓐ **They emit a loud, low frequency sound that is able to travel as much as 100 miles under water.**
Ⓑ **They use tiny whale telephones.**
Ⓒ **They send a high frequency sound that only other whales are able to hear.**
Ⓓ **None of the above**

All matter, which makes up all things, can be changed in two ways: chemically and physically. Both chemical and physical changes affect the state of matter. Physical changes are those that do not change the make-up or identity of the matter. For example, clay will bend or flatten if squeezed, but it will still be clay. Changing the shape of clay is a physical change and does not change the matter's identity. Chemical changes turn the matter into a new kind of matter with different properties. For example, when paper is burned, it becomes ash and will never be paper again. The difference between them is that physical changes are temporary or only last for a little while, and chemical changes are permanent, which means they last forever. Physical and chemical changes both affect the state of matter.

Question Number: 5

Which sentence below explains the concept of physical change?

Ⓐ **Physical change occurs when matter goes through a reaction that yields matter with a new physical makeup.**
Ⓑ **Physical change occurs when a person gains or loses weight.**
Ⓒ **Physical change is change that occurs naturally and affects the state of matter.**
Ⓓ **Physical change is change that does not change the chemical makeup of matter.**

Question Number: 6

Which sentence below explains the concept of chemical change?

Ⓐ Chemical change is change that does not change the chemical makeup of matter.
Ⓑ Chemical changes occur when a reaction takes place that changes the matter into a new kind of matter.
Ⓒ Chemical change occurs when someone mixes unknown chemicals in a beaker.
Ⓓ Chemical change occurs when clay is flattened or squeezed.

Question Number: 7

What is the primary difference between physical and chemical change?

Ⓐ Physical changes affect the state of matter, while chemical changes do not.
Ⓑ Chemical changes are temporary, while chemical changes are permanent.
Ⓒ Physical changes are temporary, whicle chemical changes are permanent.
Ⓓ All of the above

Lewis and Clark Enlist Help

Sacagawea, also spelled Sacajawea, is best known for her role in assisting Meriwether Lewis and William Clark in their expedition to explore the American West. They set out on their journey on May 14, 1804 from near what is now Wood River, Illinois; but it was that winter in South Dakota when they met Sacagawea. They reached the Pacific Ocean on the coast of Oregon in November 1805.

This journey was an historic and unprecidented exploration of what is now the American West. In those days it was a new frontier full of unknown native people and treacherous terrain. Without the help of someone who knew the land, Lewis and Clark may not have made it to the Pacific.

Sacagawea was the young Shoshone wife of a French-Canadian fur trapper named Toussaint Charbonneau. Together, she and her husband served as interpreters, guides, and negotiators for Lewis and Clark. Their friendship with Clark was so strong that they returned to settle in his home-town of St. Louis when the expedition was over. Clark even became the guardian of her children after her death.

Question Number: 8

Which of the following sentences best explains how important Sacagawea was to Lewis and Clark's expedition?

Ⓐ Sacagawea was a member of the Shoshone tribe of Native Americans.
Ⓑ Because they were travelling unknown territory, they needed the help of a person who knew about the people they would encounter and the land they would navigate.
Ⓒ Sacagawea could not have aided the Lewis and Clark expedition without the help of her husband, who was an experienced fur trapper.
Ⓓ None of the above

There are many theories about how dinosaurs came to be extinct, and scientists do not all agree about what may have happened. The most recent theory argues that a giant meteorite crashed into the earth, kicking up enough dust and debris that the Sun's rays did not reach Earth for a very long time, preventing plants from producing their own food via photosynthesis. In turn, plant-eaters died for lack of food, and then meat-eaters followed.

The other leading theory says that dinosaurs died out when the Earth went through a period of time when many volcanoes were erupting. As in the meteorite theory, it is thought that the volcanoes spewed enough volcanic ash that the Sun's rays were blocked, causing plant and animal life to perish.

Question Number: 9

How can lack of sunlight cause animals to become extinct?

Ⓐ **It disrupts the food chain starting with producers. If plants die out, then plant-eaters have nothing to eat. If plant-eaters starve and die out, then meat-eaters have nothing to eat and also die.**

Ⓑ **Dinosaurs became extinct because of widespread volcanic eruptions that blocked sunlight from reaching Earth. When this happened, plants died, beginning a disruption of the food chain that dinosaurs didn't survive.**

Ⓒ **One theory suggests a meteorite caused dinosaur extinction, while another claims widespread volcanic eruptions caused the animals to die. Both theories, however, center around the idea that plants did not get needed sunlight and plant-eating and meat-eating animals died as a result.**

Ⓓ **None of the Above**

Question Number: 10

Do all scientests agree about how dinosaurs became extinct?

Ⓐ **No. The text explains that there are many theories on dinosaur extinction and describes two of them.**
Ⓑ **No. Some scientists believe dinosaurs died when a giant meteorite crashed into earth, while others blame extraterrestrials.**
Ⓒ **Yes. The scientific community has debated several possibilities, and they agree that dinosaurs died out as the result of widespread volcanic eruptions.**
Ⓓ **All of the above**

What Does it Mean? (RI.4.4)

The blue whale is quite an extraordinary creature. To begin with, it is a mammal that lives its entire life in the ocean. The size of its body is amazing. This whale can grow up to 98 feet long and weigh as much as 200 tons, making it the largest known animal to have ever existed. Its body is long and elegantly tapered, unlike other whales which have a rounder, stockier build. Their build, along with their extreme size, gives them a unique appearance and the ability to move more gracefully and at greater speeds than one might imagine. They can reach speeds up to 31 mph for short periods of time. Their normal traveling speed is around 12 mph, but they slow to 3.1 mph when feeding. Although they are extremely large animals, they eat small shrimp-like creatures called krill. Since the krill are so small, the blue whale eats about four tons daily as they swim deep in the ocean.

Unlike other whales that live in small, close-knit groups called pods, blue whales live and travel alone or with one other whale. While traveling through the ocean, they surface to breathe air into their lungs through blowholes. They emerge from the ocean, spewing water out of their blowhole, roll, and reenter the water with a grand splash of their large tail. They make loud, deep, and rumbling low frequency sounds that travel great distances, which allow them to communicate with other whales as far as 100 miles away. Their cries can be felt as much as heard. Their resonating call makes them the loudest animal on Earth. If you ever have the opportunity to see or hear a blue whale, it will be an experience you will not soon forget.

Question Number: 1

What is the meaning of the word resonating?

Ⓐ low
Ⓑ loud
Ⓒ silent
Ⓓ quiet

Have you ever wondered what happened to the dinosaurs that once roamed the Earth? Well, scientists have developed several theories throughout the years. One such theory is that a gigantic meteorite crashed into our planet, causing a massive dust cloud to cover the Earth. The dust cloud was so enormous that it blocked the rays of the Sun from reaching Earth. This caused all of the plants to die, which lead to the herbivores to die off. Subsequently, the large carnivores also died, leaving the planet with no dinosaurs.

Question Number: 2

What is the meaning of the word herbivore?

Ⓐ A type of plant
Ⓑ An animal that eats only plants
Ⓒ A type of storm
Ⓓ An animal that eats only meat

Question Number: 3

What is the meaning of the word carnivores?

Ⓐ **A type of plant**
Ⓑ **An animal that eats only plants**
Ⓒ **A type of storm**
Ⓓ **An animal that eats only meat**

Beatrice was so excited. This was truly a special day for her. She looked down and saw that her cup was sparkling with clean and cold water. She couldn't believe it was real as she had never seen water like that before. She slowly took a sip and it tasted so fresh. Her mother always told her how important water is.

The only way that Beatrice was able to get her water in the past was from the dirty water in a ditch not far from her home. Otherwise, they would have to walk for miles to reach other areas that had water. The water there wasn't very clean, either. In fact, most of the time, this water had a horrible smell and was murky in color. Beatrice and her family knew it wasn't great, but they didn't have any choice. The water that they drank was contaminated and made Beatrice feel sick often.

The water they mostly use is from streams, rivers, and lakes and is used for cooking, taking baths, and washing clothes. This water is contaminated from chemicals in the products they use and can cause diseases, such as typhus, cholera, dysentery, and malaria.

Question Number: 4

How would you explain the phrase "murky in color"?

Ⓐ **vague and confused**
Ⓑ **bright and clear**
Ⓒ **obscure and thick with mist**
Ⓓ **dark, dingy, and cloudy**

In the United States today, we are starting to see more and more of a problem with children who are overweight. Doctors and even the President's wife are trying to do something about it. They are recommending healthier foods and that children get daily vigorous exercise. They also recommend that children go outside and do things instead of sitting in front of the tv. They have suggested that children get at least an hour of exercise a day by doing things like jumping rope or cycling, or anything else that makes their hearts beat faster. This kind of exercise is known as aerobic exercise. Something else they recommend is for children to do exercises that strengthen the bones and muscles. There are lots of ways children can do this. One way is running.

Question Number: 5

What is the meaning of vigorous in the above text?

Ⓐ slow
Ⓑ growing well
Ⓒ energetic, forceful
Ⓓ weak

People who travel on business are usually reimbursed for their travel expenses; that is, they are repaid for money they have spent for the company.

Question Number: 6

What word in the sentence above helps you understand what reimburse means?

Ⓐ expenses
Ⓑ representatives
Ⓒ repaid
Ⓓ business

Many years ago there were no self-serve grocery stores unlike today. Shoppers were served by clerks who chose everything for them. When the first self-serve market was opened, no one thought that it would be successful. Owners of the full-service grocery stores laughed at the idea and said the public would probably boycott the stores.

But Clarence Saunders, the man who came up with this new idea, thought he could save some money by having shoppers help themselves from the open shelves.

He was warned by many of his competitors that customers would boycott his new type of grocery store and put him out of business.

Question Number: 7

What is the meaning of the word boycott in the above text?

Ⓐ to only go to this store and shop there
Ⓑ to get a lot of money
Ⓒ to lose a lot of money
Ⓓ to refuse to buy something

We get a lot of copra from the Malay Peninsula. Copra is dried coconut meat which is used for making coconut oil. We use coconut oil for cooking and as an ingredient many beauty products.

Question Number: 8

Which words in the above text help to understand the meaning of copra?

Ⓐ **coconut oil**
Ⓑ **coconut meat**
Ⓒ **Malay Peninsula**
Ⓓ **None of the above**

The first review of *Despicable Me* was <u>favorable</u>. Many people attended and enjoyed the movie.

Question Number: 9

What is the meaning of the underlined word?

Ⓐ **clear**
Ⓑ **negative**
Ⓒ **positive**
Ⓓ **unsure**

Beautiful seashells that are washed ashore on beaches by ocean waves have always fascinated human beings. Shells come in a wonderful array of shapes, sizes, and colors. Shells are actually made by marine creatures to serve as their homes. Seashells are, quite simply, skeletons of mollusks. Mollusks are a class of water animals that have soft bodies and hard outer coverings, called shells. Human beings carry their bony skeletons inside and wear their soft bodies on the outside. But mollusks do just the opposite.

Shells are very <u>durable</u> and outlive the soft-bodied animals that produce them. Shells may be univalve or bivalve. Univalve shells are made up of just one unit, whereas bivalve shells have two units or two halves. Snails have univalve shells and oysters have bivalve shells. Shells protect the soft-bodied animals from rough surfaces that can harm their bodies and from predators.

Question Number: 10

What is the meaning of the underlined word ?

Ⓐ **Soft-bodied**
Ⓑ **Outlive**
Ⓒ **Protect**
Ⓓ **Tough**

How is it Written? (RI.4.5)

The blue whale is quite an extraordinary creature. To begin with, it is a mammal that lives its entire life in the ocean. The size of its body is amazing. This whale can grow up to 98 feet long and weigh as much as 200 tons, making it the largest known animal to have ever existed. Its body is long and elegantly tapered, unlike other whales which have a rounder, stockier build. Their build, along with their extreme size, gives them a unique appearance and the ability to move more gracefully and at greater speeds than one might imagine. They can reach speeds up to 31 mph for short periods of time. Their normal traveling speed is around 12 mph, but they slow to 3.1 mph when feeding. Although they are extremely large animals, they eat small shrimp-like creatures called krill. Since the krill are so small, the blue whale eats about four tons daily as they swim deep in the ocean.

Unlike other whales that live in small, close-knit groups called pods, blue whales live and travel alone or with one other whale. While traveling through the ocean, they surface to breathe air into their lungs through blowholes. They emerge from the ocean, spewing water out of their blowhole, roll, and re-enter the water with a grand splash of their large tail. They make loud, deep, and rumbling low frequency sounds that travel great distances, which allow them to communicate with other whales as far as 100 miles away. Their cries can be felt as much as heard. Their resonating call makes them the loudest animal on Earth. If you ever have the opportunity to see or hear a blue whale, it will be an experience you will not soon forget.

Question Number: 1

The author used which text structure when writing this passage?

Ⓐ **Problem and solution**
Ⓑ **Cause and effect**
Ⓒ **Sequence**
Ⓓ **Description**

Question Number: 2

A report that explains how animal cells and plant cells are alike and how they are different would be written using which of the text structures?

Ⓐ **Cause and effect**
Ⓑ **Compare and contrast**
Ⓒ **Problem and solution**
Ⓓ **Sequence or chronological**

Grandma's Chocolate Cake
1 ¾ cups all-purpose flour
2 cups white sugar
2 sticks of room temperature butter
2 eggs
¾ cup cocoa powder
1 cup milk
1 tsp. vanilla extract
1 tsp. salt

Preheat oven to 350 degrees F. Butter and flour two 8-inch cake pans.
Combine eggs, sugar, milk, vanilla extract, and butter. Beat until smooth.
Sift together the flour, salt, and cocoa powder.
Slowly add the sifted dry ingredients to the wet ingredients.
Mix until batter is smooth.
Pour the batter into the floured and greased cake pans.
Bake for 35 to 40 minutes.
Cool in pans on cooling rack for 30 minutes.
Ice cake with your favorite frosting.

Question Number: 3

Which text structure is used in the second half of the above recipe?

Ⓐ **Cause and effect**
Ⓑ **Compare and contrast**
Ⓒ **Problem and solution**
Ⓓ **Sequence**

All matter, which makes up all things, can be changed in two ways: chemically and physically. Both chemical and physical changes affect the state of matter. Physical changes are those that do not change the make-up or identity of the matter. For example, clay will bend or flatten if squeezed, but it will still be clay. Changing the shape of clay is a physical change and does not change the matter's identity. Chemical changes turn the matter into a new kind of matter with different properties. For example, when paper is burned, it becomes ash and will never be paper again. The difference between them is that physical changes are temporary or only last for a little while, and chemical changes are permanent, which means they last forever. Physical and chemical changes both affect the state of matter.

Question Number: 4

What type of structure did they use to write this paragraph?

Ⓐ **Compare and Contrast**
Ⓑ **Cause and Effect**
Ⓒ **Chronological**
Ⓓ **Problem and Solution**

Sacajawea

Sacagawea is a famous Native American from the Shoshone tribe. She became known because she helped two men, explorers named Lewis and Clark, find their way through the unexplored West. Before she was able to do that, however, she was kidnapped when she was 12 years old by an enemy Native American tribe called the Hidatsa. Then, legend has it, the chief of the Hidatsa tribe sold Sacagawea into slavery.

In 1804, she became an interpreter and guide for a group of explorers led by Lewis and Clark and she helped them find their way from the Dakotas to the Pacific Ocean. She became a famous Native American in our history for being brave and helping these men discover unknown territory.

Question Number: 5

How is the text written?

Ⓐ   **Compare and Contrast**
Ⓑ   **Cause and Effect**
Ⓒ   **Chronological**
Ⓓ   **Problem and Solution**

Question Number: 6

How could this passage be rewritten so it becomes a comparative essay?

Ⓐ   **Dates could be added to the passage.**
Ⓑ   **Excerpts from Sacagawea's personal diary could be added.**
Ⓒ   **Directions and maps from the journey could be added.**
Ⓓ   **Quotations could be added to the passage.**

Every day after school when I get home, I get certain ingredients to make myself a snack. I get the peanut butter, jelly, and bread and put everything on the counter. Peanut butter and jelly sandwiches are my favorite! Then, I take the lid off all the jars. Next, I take a big spoonful of peanut butter and spread it on one side of the bread and another big spoonful of jelly on the other. After that, I put the two pieces of bread together to make my super yummy peanut butter and jelly sandwich. I can enjoy my snack while starting my homework. It always tastes so good! Each time it seems as if it is the best peanut butter and jelly sandwich I have ever eaten.

Question Number: 7

What is the text structure of the above passage?

Ⓐ   **Cause and Effect**
Ⓑ   **Compare and contrast**
Ⓒ   **Problem and Solution**
Ⓓ   **Chronological**

Question Number: 8

If the title of an essay was, "Should Students Be Allowed to Have Cell Phones in Elementary School?" what type of writing will it be?

Ⓐ Comparative
Ⓑ Informative
Ⓒ Narrative
Ⓓ Persuasive

Question Number: 9

If the title of an essay was, "Allowing Students to have Cell Phones in Elementary Versus Middle Schools" what type of writing will it be?

Ⓐ Comparative
Ⓑ Informative
Ⓒ Narrative
Ⓓ Persuasive

Question Number: 10

If the title of an essay was, "The Pros and Cons of Wearing School Uniforms," what type of writing will it be?

Ⓐ Comparative
Ⓑ Informative
Ⓒ Narrative
Ⓓ Persuasive

Comparing Different Versions of the Same Event (RI.4.6)

The Parade: A Firsthand Account

When I got there I was dressed from head to toe in sparkly sequins and itchy tights, and I held my baton like a pro. I lined up with others in my squad and we began marching through the streets while the marching band played in front of us. I saw the crowds of people waving and smiling as we passed. Their happy faces made me feel somehow less cold, but by the second mile those happy faces could not soothe the blisters on my feet. I threw my twirling baton into the air, and this time I did not catch it. In fact, when I turned to retrieve it, I tripped the girl behind me and caused quite a situation. I was so embarrassed that I contemplated never showing my face again.

The Parade: A Secondhand Account

I read about the Thanksgiving parade in our school newspaper today. It was held downtown last saturday morning to honor the American holiday that occurs every year on the third thursday in November. There was a marching band, floats from all the local businesses, a step team, a ballet studio, and baton twirlers. The temperature outside was forty five degrees, but the sun was shining brightly to help warm over 600 people who came out to see the parade. All in all, the parade was a huge success, and the city plans to hold it again next year.

Question Number: 1

How is the focus of the firsthand account different from the secondhand account?

Ⓐ **The firsthand account focuses on the parade itself, while the secondhand account focuses on the weather on the day of the parade.**

Ⓑ **The firsthand account has a wide focus that represents the parade as a whole, while the secondhand account is narrow and only talks about the crowd who attended the parade.**

Ⓒ **The firsthand account is more accurate, while the secondhand account is based on rumor.**

Ⓓ **The firsthand account focuses only on the personal experience of the speaker, while the secondhand account gives general information from the newspaper report about the parade.**

Question Number: 2

How are the firsthand account and the secondhand account the same?

Ⓐ **They both consider the parade a huge success.**

Ⓑ **They both give specific information about the number of people in attendance.**

Ⓒ **They both discuss the baton twirlers' sequin costumes.**

Ⓓ **They both discuss the weather, the marching band, the baton twirlers, and the crowd.**

Question Number: 3

How are the firsthand account and the secondhand account different?

Ⓐ The firsthand account is more personal and includes the speaker's feelings about the parade, while the secondhand account is more objective and includes mostly facts about the parade.

Ⓑ The firsthand account includes more details about the parade, while the secondhand account is more of a broad summary.

Ⓒ The firsthand account is true, while the secondhand account gives false information.

Ⓓ The firsthand account discusses the origins of the parade, while the secondhand account is from a newspaper.

The Inauguration of Barack Obama: A Firsthand Account

When Barack Obama was inaugurated as America's first African-American president, I was watching from my TV only a couple of miles away. It was a cold, cold, cloudy day, but thousands and thousands of people climbed on jam-packed metro train cars, and busses, or even walked across the Key Bridge from Arlington Virginia to get into Washington, D.C. I saw groups of people moving down the street outside my apartment in their puffy jackets, with homemade signs and happy faces. I wondered what they would all eat and where they would use the bathroom and spend the night. I watched from the warmth of my living room with what I imagined was a much better view of our new President taking the oath of office.

The Inauguration of Barak Obama: A Secondhand Account

Barak Obama was inaugurated as our nation's 44th president on Tuesday, January 20, 2009. It was the most attended event in Washington, D.C.'s history. Because the inauguration was held during the 200th anniversary of Abraham Lincoln's birth year, there were many nods to Lincoln throughout the event. Obama was even sworn into office on the same Bible Lincoln used when he was inaugurated.

In addition to welcoming remarks, the oath of office, and an inaugural address, there was also music by Aretha Franklin and Yo Yo Ma among others. The night was capped off by a series of innaugural balls, which the new First Family attended.

Question Number: 4

How are the two accounts similar?

Ⓐ They both detail the events of election night.

Ⓑ They both give important details about the inauguration itself.

Ⓒ They both tell true events on the day of Barack Obama's first inauguration.

Ⓓ None of the above

Question Number: 5

How are the two accounts different?

Ⓐ The details in the secondhand account may not be accurate, while the details in the firsthand account have been verified to be true.

Ⓑ The secondhand account is more personal than the firsthand account.

Ⓒ The firsthand account is longer than the secondhand account.

Ⓓ The details in the first account are limited only to what the speaker witnessed, while the secondhand account gives more specific details concerning the inauguration.

Question Number: 6

What is the difference in focus between the two accounts?

Ⓐ The first account focuses on the practical details concerning the people in attendance, while the secondhand account focuses on the details of the inauguration event.

Ⓑ The firsthand account focuses on the important details, while the secondhand account is more focused on unimportaint details.

Ⓒ The secondhand account focuses on biographical details about Obama's life, while the firsthand account focuses on details like the music that played at the inauguraion.

Ⓓ Both accounts have the same focus.

John Glenn's Return to Space: a Firsthand Account

President Bill Clinton, The White House, Washington, D. C.

Dear Mr. President,
    This is certainly a first for me, writing to a President from space, and it may be a first for you in receiving an E mail direct from an orbiting spacecraft.

    In any event, I want to personally thank you and Mrs. Clinton for coming to the Cape to see the launch. I hope you enjoyed it just half as much as we did on board.. It is truly an awesome experience from a personal standpoint, and of even greater importance for all of the great research projects we have on Discovery. The whole crew was impressed that you would be the first President to personally see a shuttle launch and asked me to include their best regards to you and Hillary. She has discussed her interest in the space program with Annie on several occasions, and I know she would like to be on a flight just like this.

    We have gone almost a third of the way around the world in the time it has taken me to write this letter, and the rest of the crew is waiting. Again, our thanks and best regards. Will try to give you a personal briefing after we return next Saturday.

Sincerely,

John Glenn

Margie S. Keller
Admin Officer
Astronaut Office
281-244-8991

John Glenn's Return to Space: a Secondhand Account

In October of 1998, John Glenn returned to space aboard the space shuttle Discovery. It was on that mission that the first American to orbit the Earth made history again by becoming the oldest man to fly in space. He was a sitting U.S. Senator from Ohio at the time. President Bill Clinton attended the launch as the first U.S. President to do so.

Question Number: 7

What is the difference in focus between the firsthand and secondhand account above?

Ⓐ The firsthand account and the secondhand account have the same focus.
Ⓑ The firsthand account is more accurate than the secondhand account.
Ⓒ The firsthand account focuses on providing information to President Bill Clinton, while the secondhand account focuses on details about John Glenn.
Ⓓ None of the above

Question Number: 8

How are the two accounts similar?

Ⓐ They both give information about President Clinton being the first U.S. President to personally see a launch.
Ⓑ They both include information about the date of the historic mission.
Ⓒ They both detail the important research being conducted on the mission.
Ⓓ None of the above

Question Number: 9

How are the two accounts different?

Ⓐ The firsthand account is a letter and tells a little bit about Glenn's personal experience, while the secondhand account is an informational paragraph and was most likely written by someone who did not even know Glenn.
Ⓑ The firsthand account discusses John Glenn's return to space in 1998, while the secondhand account discusses Glenn's first orbit around Earth in 1962.
Ⓒ The firsthand account is written in complete sentences, while the secondhand account is written in short, note-like form.
Ⓓ None of the Above

Question Number: 10

What is the difference between a firsthand account and secondhand account of an event or occurance?

Ⓐ Firsthand accounts are written by people who witness an event first, while second hand accounts are written by people who witness the event second.
Ⓑ Firsthand accounts are written by people who witnessed the event, while secondhand accounts are written by people who learned details of the event from other sources.
Ⓒ Firsthand accounts are true, while secondhand accounts are usually made up.
Ⓓ All of the above

Using Text Features to Gather Information (RI.4.7)

There are four types of tissues that are formed as cells join together to function as a group. Each type of tissue has a distinctive structure and performs a specific job. Muscle tissue is made up of long and narrow muscle cells. Muscle tissue makes your body parts move by contracting and relaxing. Connective tissue is what holds up your body and connects its parts together. Bone is made up of connective tissue. Nerve tissue is made up of long nerve cells that branch through your body and carry messages throughout the body. Epithelial tissue is made of wide, flat epithelial cells. This tissue lines the surfaces inside the body and forms the outer layer of the skin. Groups of tissues join together to form the organs in our body such as the heart, liver, lungs, brain, and kidneys, just to name a few. Subsequently these organs work together to form our body systems. Each system works in complete coordination with one another, as well as with the other systems of the body.

Muscle Tissue	Connective Tissue	Nerve Tissue	Epithelial Tissue
- long, narrow cells - contracts and relaxes causing movement	- holds up the body - connects body parts together	- long cells - carries messages throughout the body	- wide, flat cells - lines inside surfaces - forms outer skin layer

Question Number: 1

How does the chart help the reader understand the functions of each of the four types of tissues?

Ⓐ It adds details not mentioned in the text so the reader can gather more information.
Ⓑ It elaborates on details mentioned in the text.
Ⓒ It changes some of the details mentioned in the text.
Ⓓ It clarifies the details mentioned in the text by categorizing them by tissue type.

Question Number: 2

Which types of tissue have similarly shaped cells?

Ⓐ Epithelial tissue and connective tissue
Ⓑ Muscle tissue and connective tissue
Ⓒ Connective tissue and nerve tissue
Ⓓ Muscle tissue and nerve tissue

Question Number: 3

To help the reader visualize what each of tissue looks like, what would be the BEST visual aid to include with this text?

Ⓐ A drawing of the heart, liver, lungs, brain, and kidneys
Ⓑ Microscopic views of each type of tissue
Ⓒ A diagram of a nerve cell
Ⓓ A chart providing information about each type of tissue

Most people refer to koalas as koala bears, but they are not bears at all. They are actually marsupials and are in the same family as the wombat. Koalas live in eucalyptus forests in Eastern and South-Eastern Australia. Adult koalas are one of only three mammals that can survive on a diet of eucalyptus leaves. These leaves contain 50% water, requiring them to seldom drink water since they obtain it through the leaves.

Since the koala is a marsupial, the baby crawls into the mother's pouch as soon as it is born. Baby koalas are called "joeys." When they are born, they are blind, hairless, and less than one inch long. They remain in their mother's pouch for the next six months, feeding first on the mother's milk and then on a substance called "pap" in addition to the mother's milk. Joeys continue to take their mother's milk until they are a year old. The young koala will remain with its mother until the appearance of another joey in the mother's pouch.

Question Number: 4

Which picture or illustration would not help the reader understand the above text and should not be included?

Ⓐ **A picture of an adult koala**
Ⓑ **A picture of a newborn 'joey'**
Ⓒ **A picture of a polar bear**
Ⓓ **A map showing areas where koalas are found naturally**

The digestive system is made up of the esophagus, stomach, liver, gall bladder, pancreas, large and small intestines, appendix, and rectum. Digestion actually begins in the mouth when food is chewed and mixed with saliva. Muscles in the esophagus push food into the stomach where it mixes with digestive juices. While in the stomach, food is broken down into nutrients and turned into a thick liquid. The food then moves into the small intestines where more digestive juices complete the breaking down of the food. It is in the small intestines that nutrients are absorbed into the blood and carried throughout the body. The leftover material that is unusable by the body moves into the large intestines where the body absorbs the water that is contained in it before passing it from the body through the rectum.

Question Number: 5

What visual aid should be included with the above text to enhance student understand -ing?

Ⓐ **A diagram of the digestive system**
Ⓑ **A diagram of the mouth**
Ⓒ **A diagram of food**
Ⓓ **A diagram of stomach tissue**

Sacajawea

Sacagawea is a famous Native American from the Shoshone tribe. She became known because she helped two men, explorers named Lewis and Clark, find their way through the unexplored west. Before she was able to do that, however, she was kidnapped when she was 12 years old by an enemy Native American tribe called the Hidatsa. Then, legend has it, that the chief of the Hidatsa tribe sold Sacagawea into slavery.

In 1804, she became an interpreter and guide for a group of explorers led by Lewis and Clark, and she helped them find their way from the Dakotas to the Pacific Ocean. She became a famous Native American in our history for being brave and helping these men discover unknown territory.

Question Number: 6

Which of the pictures below best represents what is being explained in the text?

Ⓐ

Ⓑ

Ⓒ

Ⓓ **None of the above**

The blue whale is quite an extraordinary creature. To begin with, it is a mammal that lives its entire life in the ocean. The size of its body is amazing. This whale can grow up to 98 feet long and weigh as much as 200 tons, making it the largest known animal to have ever existed. Its body is long and elegantly tapered, unlike other whales which have a rounder, stockier build. Their build, along with their extreme size, gives them a unique appearance and the ability to move more gracefully and at greater speeds than one might imagine. They can reach speeds up to 31 mph for short periods of time. Their normal traveling speed is around 12 mph, but they slow to 3.1 mph when feeding. Although they are extremely large animals, they eat small shrimp-like creatures called krill. Since the krill are so small, the blue whale eats about four tons daily as they swim deep in the ocean.

Unlike other whales that live in small, close-knit groups called pods, blue whales live and travel alone or with one other whale. While traveling through the ocean, they surface to breathe air into their lungs through blowholes. They emerge from the ocean, spewing water out of their blowhole, roll, and reenter the water with a grand splash of their large tail. They make loud, deep, and rumbling low frequency sounds that travel great distances, which allow them to communicate with other whales as far as 100 miles away. Their cries can be felt as much as heard. Their resonating call makes them the loudest animal on Earth. If you ever have the opportunity to see or hear a blue whale, it will be an experience you will not soon forget.

Question Number: 7

What would be an important illustration or picture to include with this article?

Ⓐ **A picture of the ocean**
Ⓑ **A picture of a pod of whales**
Ⓒ **A picture of an adult blue whale**
Ⓓ **A picture of a whaling ship**

The following excerpt is from the November 12, 1892 edition of "Golden Days" magazine. It explains how condensed milk was made:
The processes employed are very simple, the fresh milk being put into a great copper tank with a steam jacket. While it is being heated sugar is added, and the mixture is then drawn off into a vacuum tank, where evaporation is produced by heat.

The vacuum tank will hold, perhaps, nine thousand quarts. It has a glass window at the top, through which the operator in charge looks from time to time. He can tell by the appearance of the milk when the time has arrived to shut off the steam, and this must be done at just the right moment, else the batch will be spoiled.

Next the condensed milk is drawn into forty-quart cans, which are set in very cold spring water, where they are made to revolve rapidly by a mechanical contrivance in order that their contents may cool evenly.

When the water does not happen to be cold enough, ice is put in to bring it down to the proper temperature. Finally the tin cans of market size are filled with the milk by a machine, which pours into each one exactly sixteen ounces automatically, one girl shoving the cans beneath the spout, while another removes them as fast as they are filled.

Question Number: 8

Which text feature would be most helpful for the reader to understand the process of making condensed milk?

Ⓐ **A numbered list of steps with illustrations for each step**
Ⓑ **A timeline of the events in the process**
Ⓒ **A map of where evaporated milk was made in 1892**
Ⓓ **None of the above**

BETWEEN WOOD AND FIELD. Arrangement of wall tents with flys, set up with stakes.

THE TENT "GREEN." Conical wall tents accommodating eight cots. Not easy to put up and give little head room.

Well-built floors keep out ground damp, and make level and steady supports.

Question Number: 9

These photographs and captions are most likely included in which of the following texts?

Ⓐ **A recipe book for outdoorsmen**
Ⓑ **A guide to city life**
Ⓒ **A guide to Girl Scout camps**
Ⓓ **A fishing guide**

Catepillar feeding on a milkweed leaf as it prepares to begin its transition

Catepillar hung up for the change to the chrysalis phase

The transition stage

The chrysalis

Question Number: 10

What would these photographs and captions be most helpful in explaining?

Ⓐ **All about plants**
Ⓑ **A very hungry caterpillar**
Ⓒ **How a catepillar begins its transformation into a butterfly**
Ⓓ **None of the above**

Finding the Evidence (RI.4.8)

The blue whale is quite an extraordinary creature. To begin with, it is a mammal that lives its entire life in the ocean. The size of its body is amazing. This whale can grow up to 98 feet long and weigh as much as 200 tons, making it the largest known animal to have ever existed. Its body is long and elegantly tapered, unlike other whales which have a rounder, stockier build. Their build, along with their extreme size, gives them a unique appearance and the ability to move more gracefully and at greater speeds than one might imagine. They can reach speeds up to 31 mph for short periods of time. Their normal traveling speed is around 12 mph, but they slow to 3.1 mph when feeding. Although they are extremely large animals, they eat small shrimp-like creatures called krill. Since the krill are so small, the blue whale eats about four tons daily as they swim deep in the ocean.

Unlike other whales that live in small, close-knit groups called pods, blue whales live and travel alone or with one other whale. While traveling through the ocean, they surface to breathe air into their lungs through blowholes. They emerge from the ocean, spewing water out of their blowhole, roll, and reenter the water with a grand splash of their large tail. They make loud, deep, and rumbling low frequency sounds that travel great distances, which allow them to communicate with other whales as far as 100 miles away. Their cries can be felt as much as heard. Their resonating call makes them the loudest animal on Earth. If you ever have the opportunity to see or hear a blue whale, it will be an experience you will not soon forget.

Question Number: 1

Which statement did the writer of this passage use to support his opinion that the size of a blue whale's body is amazing?

Ⓐ The blue whale is quite an extraordinary creature.
Ⓑ Its body is long and elegantly tapered, unlike other whales which have a rounder, stockier body.
Ⓒ This whale can grow up to 98 feet long and weigh as much as 200 tons, making it the largest known animal to have ever existed.
Ⓓ Their build, along with their extreme size, gives them a unique appearance and the ability to move gracefully and at greater speeds than one might imagine.

Question Number: 2

What evidence does the author provide in the second paragraph that supports the fact that whales communicate with one another?

Ⓐ Blue whales live and travel alone or with one other whale.
Ⓑ They emerge from the ocean, spewing water out of their blowhole, roll over, and re-enter the water with a grand splash of their tail.
Ⓒ They make loud, deep, and rumbling low-frequency sounds that travel great distances, which allow them to communicate with other whales as much as 100 miles away.
Ⓓ Their cries can be felt as much as heard.

2362 West Main Street
Jojo, TX 98456

June 16, 2010

Dear Mr. Seymour:

I ordered a Magic Racing Top from your Company. The toy was delivered to me today in a package that was badly damaged. I took a picture of the box before I opened it, which I am sending to you as proof of damage. The toy inside was broken due, I'm sure, to the damage to the package during shipping.

This toy was to be a gift for my friend's birthday. There is not enough time before his party to wait on a replacement toy; therefore, I no longer need the toy. I would like for you to refund my money. If you would like for me to return the broken toy, please send a prepaid shipping label.

Thank you for handling this matter for me. I look forward to hearing from you and hope we can satisfactorily resolve this problem.

Sincerely,
Tim West

Question Number: 3

What evidence does the writer of this letter offer to support his claim that the package arrived damaged?

Ⓐ **The toy was broken.**
Ⓑ **He wanted a replacement or a refund.**
Ⓒ **He is sending a picture of the damaged package.**
Ⓓ **He wants to satisfactorily resolve the problem.**

Question Number: 4

The author does not want a replacement toy. What reason does he give for not wanting a replacement?

Ⓐ **The package was damaged during shipping.**
Ⓑ **The toy was a gift, and there is not enough time to ship a replacement.**
Ⓒ **The toy is broken.**
Ⓓ **He requests a prepaid shipping label to return the toy.**

Digestive System

The digestive system is made up of the esophagus, stomach, liver, gall bladder, pancreas, large and small intestines, appendix, and rectum. Digestion actually begins in the mouth when food is chewed and mixed with saliva. Muscles in the esophagus push food into the stomach where it mixes with digestive juices. While in stomach, food is broken down into nutrients and turns into a thick liquid. The food then moves into the small intestines where more digestive juices complete the breaking down of the food. It is in the small intestines that nutrients are absorbed into the blood and carried throughout the body. The leftover material that is unusable by the body moves into the large intestines where the body absorbs the water that is contained before passing from the body through the rectum.

Question Number: 5

What evidence does the writer provide to support the fact that everything eaten is not used by the body for nutrients?

Ⓐ **Digestion actually begins in the mouth when food is chewed and mixed with saliva.**
Ⓑ **The food then moves into the small intestines where more digestive juices complete the breaking down of the food.**
Ⓒ **It is in the small intestines that nutrients are absorbed into the blood and carried throughout the body.**
Ⓓ **The leftover material that is unusable by the body moves into the large intestines where the body absorbs the water that is contained before passing from the body through the rectum.**

Smoking is a nasty habit. It not only damages your health, but it also affects the way you look and even smell. People who smoke have horrible breath that smells like a dirty ashtray, but it is not only their breath that smells bad. Their clothes and hair also smell like smoke, and if this isn't bad enough, smoking causes their teeth to turn yellow.

Question Number: 6

Above is a section from a persuasive essay written to encourage people not to smoke. What evidence does the writer provide that supports the claim that smoking affects the way you look?

Ⓐ **Smoking is a nasty habit.**
Ⓑ **People who smoke have horrible breath.**
Ⓒ **Their clothes and hair smell like smoke.**
Ⓓ **Smoking causes their teeth to turn yellow.**

Question Number: 7

Above is a section from a persuasive essay written to encourage people not to smoke. Which statement does NOT provide evidence that supports the claim that smoking causes you smell bad?

Ⓐ People who smoke have horrible breath that smells like a dirty ashtray.
Ⓑ Onions also may you cause you to have bad breath.
Ⓒ but it is not only their breath that smells bad
Ⓓ Their clothes and hair also smell like smoke.

Drinking alcohol and driving is a dangerous combination. This is because of the way alcohol affects the nervous system. Alcohol can make you act silly and laugh at things that are not funny. Alcohol slows down the brain. This causes the driver to have a slower reaction time and difficulty thinking, causing them to be unable to make quick, clear decisions about traffic and road conditions. In addition, alcohol's effect on the brain causes a lack of coordination. This can lead a driver to weave on and off the road or have trouble applying the brakes when needed. Any one of these reactions can easily cause a driver to have an accident that could harm or kill themselves or others.

Question Number: 8

Above is a section from a persuasive essay written to encourage people not to drink. What statement does NOT provide evidence supporting the writer's claim that drinking alcohol and driving is dangerous?

Ⓐ Alcohol can make you act silly and laugh at things that are not funny.
Ⓑ Alcohol slows down the brain.
Ⓒ Alcohol's effect on the brain causes lack of coordination.
Ⓓ This can lead a driver to weave on and off the road or have trouble applying the brakes when needed.

Dr. Johnson thinks that everyone should take responsiblility for preserving the toad species. By not mowing certain areas of our lawns, special areas of wild grass could be kept for toads. This could possibly help to preserve the species. According to Dr. Johnson, dangerous chemicals found in pesticides and fertilizers are also reasons why the species is starting to disappear. These chemicals have an effect on the food chain and can kill the insects that the toads eat. If we are able to keep a special space in our yards and stop using chemical fertilizers, Dr. Johnson believes that the toads can be saved.

Question Number: 9

What would be an appropriate title for the above text?

Ⓐ Please Stop Mowing Your Lawn
Ⓑ Don't Let Toads Disappear
Ⓒ Please Stop Using Fertiilizers
Ⓓ Dr. Johnson and the Toad

In the United States today, we are starting to see more and more of a problem with children who are overweight. Doctors and even the President's wife are trying to do something about it. They are recommending healthier foods and that children get daily exercise. They also recommend that children go outside and do things instead of sitting in front of the tv. They have suggested that children get at least an hour of exercise a day by doing things like jumping rope or cycling, or anything else that makes their hearts beat faster. This kind of exercise is known as aerobic exercise. Something else they recommend is for children to do exercises that strengthen the bones and muscles. There are lots of ways children can do this. One way is running.

Question Number: 10

What is the main idea of the above text?

Ⓐ **Doctors want you to move.**
Ⓑ **It is very important for kids to exercise daily.**
Ⓒ **Jumping and other activities help make your bones strong.**
Ⓓ **Any physical exercise helps make your heart beat stronger.**

Integrating Information (RI.4.9)

On the Trail: an Outdoor Book for Girls by Adelia Beard and Lina Beard

For any journey, by rail or by boat, one has a general idea of the direction to be taken, the character of the land or water to be crossed, and of what one will find at the end. So it should be in striking the trail. Learn all you can about the path you are to follow. Whether it is plain or obscure, wet or dry; where it leads; and its length, measured more by time than by actual miles. A smooth, even trail of five miles will not consume the time and strength that must be expended upon a trail of half that length which leads over uneven ground, varied by bogs and obstructed by rocks and fallen trees, or a trail that is all up-hill climbing.

How to Camp Out by John M. Gould

Think over and decide whether you will walk, go horseback, sail, camp out in one place, or what you will do; then learn what you can of the route you propose to go over, or the ground where you intend to camp for the season. If you think of moving through or camping in places unknown to you, it is important to learn whether you can buy provisions and get lodgings along your route. See some one, if you can, who has been where you think of going, [Pg 10]and put down in a note-book all he tells you that is important.

Question Number: 1

Which sentence below integrates information from the above texts?

Ⓐ **Hiking over bogs or fallen trees is harder than hiking an even, unobscured trail.**
Ⓑ **You should talk to someone who has been where you plan to go so you can get information and tips that will be helpful in planning your camping trip.**
Ⓒ **Hiking over uneven land will take longer than going the same distance over flat land.**
Ⓓ **When planning a camping trip, it is important to plan by considering both the terrain of the trail you will travel and whether you will walk or ride on horseback.**

Question Number: 2

Which paragraph below integrates information from the above texts?

Ⓐ **Camping is terribly difficult, and only true experts should attempt to camp overnight.**
Ⓑ **If you intend to camp somewhere you've never been, you should learn everything you can about the trail. Find out what the land is like and where you can buy supplies along the way.**
Ⓒ **Only boys can go on long camping trips across bogs or uneven terrain.**
Ⓓ **You should always take a notebook on your camping trips to write about your trip and draw pictures of plants and animals you see.**

Question Number: 3

Which pair of sentences shows similar information found in both texts?

Ⓐ "Learn all you can about the path you are to follow."
"Learn what you can of the route you propose to go over."

Ⓑ "So it should be in striking the trail."
"Think over and decide whether you will walk, go horseback, sail, camp out in one place, or what you will do…"

Ⓒ "A smooth, even trail of five miles will not consume the time and strength that must be expended upon a trail of half that length which leads over uneven ground…"
"… It is important to learn whether you can buy provisions and get lodgings along your route."

Ⓓ All of the above

The Amazing Peacock

Did you know that the term, "peacock" really only refers to the male of its species? A female pea-fowl is actually called a "peahen." Peacocks are native to India and other parts of Southeast Asia and are known for their brilliantly colored plumage. Their bodies can be thirty-five to fifty inches, while their beautiful tails can be as long as five feet! People admire peacocks for their beautiful feathers, but they also serve a purpose for the birds. The peacocks' tails help peahens choose their mates!

The Peafowl and It's Magnificent Tail

Peafowl are glorious animals and have long been admired by humans for their beautiful, brightly colored tail feathers. Their tails do not reach their full length until the peacock is four or five years old. When that happens, the peacock will strut day after day in hopes of attracting a mate. Pea-fowl are actually a kind of pheasant. Some are natives of India, while others come from Sri Lanka, Myanmar (Burma), or Java. Peafowl are some of the largest flying birds around!

Question Number: 4

Which paragraph below integrates information from both texts above?

Ⓐ The peafowl, more commonly known as the peacock, has beautiful tail feathers. Those feathers can grow to be around five feet long, but their growth usually does not peak until the peacock is four or five years old.

Ⓑ Peacocks are wonderful creatures. They come from India, and their bodies can grow to be thirty-five to fifty inches long.

Ⓒ Peacocks like to strut around all day with their beautiful feathers spread wide for all to see. This is what helps them to find a mate.

Ⓓ None of the above

Question Number: 5

Which sentence below integrates information from both texts above?

Ⓐ Peacocks have been admired by humans for over a thousand years because their tail feathers are so beautiful.
Ⓑ "Peafowl" actually refers to both the male and female of its species, while "peacock" is the correct term for the male only.
Ⓒ Peacocks are enormous.
Ⓓ With bodies as big as thirty-five to fifty inches and tails as long as five feet, peacocks are some of the largest flying birds you will ever see.

Sacagawea

Sacagawea is a famous Native American from the Shoshone tribe. She became known because she helped two men, explorers named Lewis and Clark, find their way through the unexplored west. Before she was able to do that, however, she was kidnapped when she was 12 years old by an enemy Native American tribe called the Hidatsa. Then, legend has it, that the chief of the Hidatsa tribe sold Sacagawea into slavery.

In 1804, she became an interpreter and guide for a group of explorers led by Lewis and Clark, and she helped them find their way from the Dakotas to the Pacific Ocean. She became a famous Native American in our history for being brave and helping these men discover unknown territory.

Lewis and Clark Enlist Help

Sacagawea, also spelled *Sacajawea*, is best known for her role in assisting Meriwether Lewis and William Clark in their expedition to explore the American West. They set out on their journey on May 14, 1804 from near what is now Wood River, Illinois; but it was that winter in South Dakota that they met Sacagawea. They reached the Pacific Ocean on the coast of Oregon in November 1805.

Sacagawea was the young Shoshone wife of a French-Canadian fur trapper named Toussaint Charbonneau. Together, she and her husband served as an interpreters, guides, and negotiators for Lewis and Clark. Their friendship with Clark was so strong that they returned to settle in his hometown of St. Louis when the expedition was over. Clark even became the guardian of her children after her death.

Question Number: 6

Which of the following sentences integrates information from both texts above?

Ⓐ Despite being kidnapped and sold into slavery at the age of 12, Sacagawea went on to guide and befriend Meriwether Lewis and William Clark on their journey of exploration from South Dakota to the Pacific Ocean in Oregon.

Ⓑ Sacagawea is a famous and brave Shoshone Indian who helped guide Lewis and Clark on their journey to find new territory.

Ⓒ Sacagawea developed such a strong bond with William Clark that after the expedition she moved to his city and even left her children in his care when she died.

Ⓓ None of the above

Question Number: 7

Which of the following sentences integrates information from both texts above?

Ⓐ Sacagawea was a Shoshone princess who very slyly took charge of one of the most famous explorations in American History.

Ⓑ Sacagawea did serve as interpreter and guide, but it was merely her presence that showed William's and Clark's peaceful intentions when the expedition encountered new tribes.

Ⓒ At twelve, Sacagawea was kidnapped and sold to a French-Canadian man; but she eventually married that fur trapper, Toussaint Charbonneau, and together they became part of an expedition that will live on in history.

Ⓓ All of the above

Question Number: 8

Which of the following sentences integrates information from both texts above?

Ⓐ Sacagawea was a member of the Shoshone tribe of Native Americans.

Ⓑ Sacagawea was brave because she was kidnapped as a child, went on a treacherous and historic journey across the American West, and also ventured to live in a new city.

Ⓒ Sacagawea could not have aided the Lewis and Clark expedition without the help of her husband, who was an experienced fur trapper.

Ⓓ None of the above

One Theory on Dinosaur Extinction

Have you ever wondered what happened to the dinosaurs that once roamed the Earth? Well, scientists have developed several theories throughout the years. One such theory is that a gigantic meteorite crashed into our planet, causing a massive dust cloud to cover the Earth. The dust cloud was so enormous that it blocked the rays of the Sun from reaching Earth. This caused all of the plants to die, which led to the herbivores dying. Subsequently, the large carnivores also died, leaving the planet with no dinosaurs.

Dinosaur Die-out: Competing Theories

There are many theories about how dinosaurs came to be extinct, and scientists do not all agree about what may have happened. The most recent theory argues that a giant meteorite crashed into the earth, kicking up enough dust and debris that the Sun's rays did not reach Earth for a very long time, causing the plants and animals to die.

The other leading theory says that dinosaurs died out when the Earth went through a period of time when many volcanoes were erupting. As in the meteorite theory, it is thought that the volcanoes spewed enough volcanic ash that the Sun's rays were blocked, causing plant and animal life to perish.

Question Number: 9

Which of the following paragraphs integrates information from both of the above texts?

Ⓐ **Dinosaurs are thought to have become extinct 65 million years ago, but some scientists theorize that they are still roaming remote parts of the Amazon Rainforest.**

Ⓑ **Dinosaurs became extinct because of widespread volcanic eruptions that blocked sunlight from reaching Earth. When this happened, plants died, beginning a disruption of the food chain that dinosaurs didn't survive.**

Ⓒ **One theory suggests a meteorite caused dinosaur extinction, while another claims widespread volcanic eruptions caused the animals to die. Both theories, however, center around the idea that plants did not get needed sunlight and plant-eating and meat-eating animals died as a result.**

Ⓓ **None of the Above**

Question Number: 10

Which of the following sentences integrates information from both of the above texts?

Ⓐ Several theories exist about how dinosaurs became extinct; but the two main theories are that either a meteorite crashing into Earth or a series of massive volcanic eruptions caused the animals to die out.

Ⓑ Dinosaurs may have become extinct because a giant meteorite crashed into the Earth somewhere near the Gulf of Mexico, but scientists are not sure.

Ⓒ If producers are unable to get sunlight, photosynthesis can't take place. This means plant-eating animals do not have food, thus meaning that meat-eating animals will not have food either.

Ⓓ All of the above

End of Reading: Informational Text

Answer Key and Detailed Explanations

Reading: Informational Text

It's All in the Details (RI.4.1)

Question No.	Answer	Detailed Explanation
1	D	The fourth answer choice is correct. The author says the Ostrich, "cannot fly," and that, "it can travel faster by running." Traveling faster is an advantage for the Ostrich.
2	D	The fourth answer choice is correct. By saying, "one of their favorite companions," the author implies the Ostrich has many companions. The Ostrich is not shy and solitary if it has many companions.
3	A	"Solitary" means alone. The first answer choice is correct because the statement contrasts the blue whale's behavior with the behavior of other whales that live in pods.
4	D	The fourth answer choice is correct because it mentions the advantage to getting friends to join. While the third answer choice does mention getting friends to join, it does not mention any benefit that would encourage the audience to recruit their friends.
5	A	The first choice is correct. While the text does make a convincing case for the theory that a meteorite crashed into the Earth, causing dinosaurs to die out, the author implies that there are other theories by saying, "<u>One</u> such theory..."
6	D	The second answer choice is correct. Paragraph 2 includes details like, "when the weather begins to get warmer after winter, these little frogs start to sing," and their song, "can be heard for miles around." Paragraph 3 also helps support her point by including details about how spring peepers "hide under fallen leaves or even in a small hole in the ground," when cold weather comes. Singing would make the peeper easy to find, while hiding would make it difficult to see one.
7	C	The third answer choice is correct. The author does not include northwestern Australia as one of the areas koalas call home.
8	B	The author writes that, "muscle tissue makes your body parts move by contracting and relaxing."

Question No.	Answer	Detailed Explanation
9	D	Microscopic views of each tissue type would show the reader exactly what each type looks like and how they are different.
10	C	The third choice is correct. Although the letter is polite, Tim West was displeased with his experience. Only dissatisfied customers ask for refunds.

The Main Idea (RI.4.2)

1	B	Option B is the correct main idea. Although each of the other options can be found in the passage they are simply details and are not the main idea.
2	A	The correct answer is A. Options B and C are incorrect statements and although option D is a correct statement, it does not support the main idea.
3	A	The first choice is correct, because it is the main idea of the passage.
4	B	The second choice is correct, because the entire passage was how Alexander figured out how to tame the horse (smartness) and how he became a great man in history (greatness).
5	C	Dumping of industrial wastes and household refuse are types of pollution.
6	B	The second choice is correct, because the passage states that shells are made by marine creatures to serve as their homes.
7	B	The second choice is correct, because the passage was about Sacagawea and the amazing things she did.
8	A	The first choice is correct because it includes what the passage was about and the most important information.
9	A	The first choice is correct, because the whole passage is about how that type of dog is unique.
10	C	Option C is the correct answer. Although each statement comes directly from the passage, only option C supports the main idea. As the sun was blocked from the dust, it killed off all plant life, leaving nothing for the dinosaurs to survive on.

Using Details to Explain the Text (RI.4.3)

Question No.	Answer	Detailed Explanation
1	C	The third answer choice is correct. The text says, "Digestion actually begins in the mouth when food is chewed and mixed with saliva."
2	D	The fourth choice is correct. The text says, "nutrients are absorbed into the blood and carried throughout the body."
3	C	The third choice is correct. The text says, "they surface to breathe air into their lungs through blowholes. They emerge from the ocean, spewing water out of their blowhole, roll, and reenter the water with a grand splash of their large tail." Choice A is false, while choice B has the order of events incorrect.
4	A	The first choice is correct. The text says, "They make loud, deep, and rumbling low frequency sounds that travel great distances, which allow them to communicate with other whales as far as 100 miles away."
5	D	The fourth choice is correct. It explains the essential idea of physical change as described in the text.
6	B	The second choice is correct. It explains the essential idea of chemical change as described in the text.
7	C	The third choice is correct. The text says, "The difference between them is that physical changes are temporary or only last for a little while, and chemical changes are permanent, which means they last forever."
8	B	Because they were travelling unknown territory, they needed the help of a person who knew about the people they would encounter and the land they would navigate.
9	A	The first choice is correct. The text says, "..the Sun's rays did not reach Earth for a very long time, preventing plants from producing their own food via photosynthesis. In turn, plant-eaters died for lack of food, and then meat-eaters followed."
10	A	The first choice is correct. The text says, "There are many theories about how dinosaurs came to be extinct." Then it goes on to describe two such theories: a meteorite collision and widespread volcanic eruptions.

What Does it Mean? (RI.4.4)

Question No.	Answer	Detailed Explanation
1	B	Resonating means loud, because the passage says that their resonating sound makes them the loudest animal on earth.
2	B	An herbivore is an animal that eats only plants. The passage gives us a clue when it said that the plants dying caused the herbivores to die.
3	D	Carnivores are animals that eat only meat.
4	D	Murky in color means dark, dingy, and cloudy. The water was very dirty and dark.
5	C	Vigorous means energetic and forceful. Exercise would be pointless if it wasn't energetic.
6	C	The word repaid is a context clue that helps us figure out what reimbursed means.
7	D	Boycott means refuse to buy something. In this case, the people would refuse to go to a store.
8	B	The second sentence tells us exactly the definition of copra.
9	C	Favorable means positive. People enjoyed it is a clue.
10	D	Durable means hardy and tough. The fact that shells often outlive the animals inside explains how tough they are.

How is it Written? (RI.4.5)

1	D	Descriptive text structures give characteristics of a particular topic in no particular order.
2	B	Compare/contrast passages tell how subjects are alike and different.
3	D	The text structure is sequence, because the steps are given in the order that they are supposed to occur.
4	A	The structure is compare/contrast, because it tells how chemical and physical changes are different.
5	C	The text structure is chronological, because it gives the events in the order that they occurred.
6	B	Adding passages from Sacagawea's personal diary would add a different perspective to the passage, allowing readers to view the information from two points of view and compare both sets of information.

Question No.	Answer	Detailed Explanation
7	D	The text structure is chronological, because it gives the events in the order that they occurred.
8	D	This is persuasive writing, because it gives an opinion and tries to get others to agree.
9	A	This is a comparative essay because it is looking at the issue of cell phones in schools from two different perspectives: elementary and middle.
10	A	This is a comparison essay because it gives both sides of the discussion of school uniforms. It compares the pros and the cons.

Comparing Different Versions of the Same Event (RI.4.6)

1	D	The fourth choice is correct. The first hand accound is by the baton twirler and is limited to her personal experiences and observations. The second hand account covers the observations about the entire parade by the reporter.
2	D	The fourth choice is correct. There is information in both texts about the weather, the marching band, the baton twirlers, and the crowd. The other answer choices only appear in one of the two accounts.
3	A	The first choice is correct. We learn in the firsthand account that the narrator is embarrassed by the events during the parade, while the secondhand account omits emotions and includes mostly facts about the parade.
4	C	The third choice is correct. The firsthand account describes how bunches of people walked down the street on their way to the inauguration, and the secondhand account gives details about the inauguration on that same day.
5	D	The fourth choice is correct. The other answer choices have no support.
6	A	The first choice is correct. It could be argued that the details in both accounts are important, and the third and fourth choices are false.
7	C	The third choice is correct. The firsthand account is a letter from John Glenn himself to then President Bill Clinton. The secondhand account gives information about John Glenn's 1998 return mission to space.
8	A	The first choice is correct. It is the only information to appear in both documents.

Question No.	Answer	Detailed Explanation
9	A	The first choice is correct. It explains how the two texts are different.
10	B	The second choice is correct. Firsthand accounts represent people's personal experiences, while secondhand accounts are told or written by those who gather the information about the event from another source.

Using Text Features to Gather Information (RI.4.7)

1	D	The fourth answer choice is correct. The chart makes the details clear by categorizing them according to tissue type. It does not add information or elaborate, but rather makes the information more concise. It does not change details.
2	D	The fourth answer choice is correct. The chart makes it easy to see that both muscle tissue and nerve tissue have long cells.
3	B	Microscopic views of each tissue type would show the reader exactly what each type looks like and how they are different.
4	C	A picture of a polar bear would not be helpful, because this passage is about koalas. Koalas are not bears.
5	A	A diagram of the digestive system would be helpful so the reader could see what the different organs look like and where they are located compared to one another.
6	A	The picture of a Native American female is appropriate since the passage is about Sacagawea.
7	C	A picture of an adult blue whale would be helpful, because the passage describes what they look like and how large they are.
8	A	The first choice is correct. Steps in a process would be most easily understood with the help of a numbered, illustrated list of steps. A timeline is meant to cover a longer time span, and a map would not help the reader understand steps in a process.
9	C	The third choice is correct. Camping is the only topic listed that would require knowledge of tents like the ones pictured.
10	C	The third answer choice is correct. The photographs show the different stages of a caterpillar going into its chrysalis in preparation to become a butterfly. The captions use words like, "change" and "transition" to make that more clear.

Finding the Evidence (RI.4.8)

Question No.	Answer	Detailed Explanation
1	C	The third choice is correct. It gives specific details about the size and weight of the blue whale's body.
2	C	The third choice tells specifically how the whales communicate.
3	C	The third choice is correct. The picture is evidence that it was broken.
4	B	The second choice is correct. In the letter, the boy states that there is not enough time before his friend's birthday for the company to send a replacement toy.
5	D	The fourth choice tells what happens to the unabsorbed nutrients.
6	D	Yellow teeth is a specific example of how smoking affects the way one looks.
7	B	Choice 3 is how onions can make you smell bad, not cigarettes.
8	A	Choice 1 has nothing to do with driving.
9	B	Don't Let Toads Disappear is an appropriate title, because the purpose of the text is to encourage people to do things to prevent toads from vanishing.
10	B	The main idea is for kids to exercise. The entire passage is about this.

Integrating Information (RI.4.9)

1	D	The fourth answer choice is correct. The first three choices include only information from one of the texts. The fourth choice integrates information from both texts.
2	B	The second choice is correct. Information from the other three choices are not found in the texts.
3	A	The first choice is correct. This is the only choice with a pair of sentences from each text that mean essentially the same thing. When doing research, one should look for similar information found in multiple texts, as this adds to its validity.
4	A	The first choice is correct. It integrates information from both texts about the growth and length of a peacock's feathers.
5	D	The fourth choice is correct. It is the only answer choice that includes information from both texts.

Question No.	Answer	Detailed Explanation
6	A	Only the first choice includes information from both texts. Choice 2 only uses information from the first passage, while choice 3 only uses information from the second passage.
7	C	The third choice is correct. The first choice is untrue, and the second choice includes information not mentioned in either text above.
8	B	The second choice is correct. It uses examples from both texts to justify bravery as a character trait for Sacagawea. The first choice is a statement of fact, rather than an integration of facts from multiple texts. The third choice is an opinion not represented in either text.
9	C	The third choice is correct. The first choice is untrue, and the second choice asserts the volcano theory as fact, disregarding any discussion of a meteorite.
10	A	The first choice is correct. It integrates information from both texts. The second choice gives additional information on only one theory, and the third choice further explains how blocked sunlight could result in dinosaur extinction.

Language

Pronouns (L.4.1.A)

Question Number: 1

Bobby and I have practice every day. The 7th graders practice first and their practice always runs long. I live closer but Bobby is on my team, so ____ walk to the games together.

Choose the correct pronoun to complete the sentence.

Ⓐ I
Ⓑ We
Ⓒ Us
Ⓓ They

Question Number: 2

We were reading outside when my father wanted us to do something fun. He told me a story about a treehouse _____ and his father built when he was younger. He knew there were pictures inside, so he asked me to bring his book inside.

Choose the correct pronoun to complete the sentence.

Ⓐ he
Ⓑ him
Ⓒ his
Ⓓ us

Question Number: 3

I would like for you to meet Jamie. _____ is my best friend.

Choose the correct pronoun to complete the sentence.

Ⓐ He
Ⓑ Him
Ⓒ Its
Ⓓ Their

Question Number: 4

My dogs love to play with _____ squeaky toys.

Choose the correct pronoun to complete the sentence.

Ⓐ his
Ⓑ its
Ⓒ their
Ⓓ them

Question Number: 5

The little girl put _____ doll in the toy box before going to bed.

Choose the correct pronoun to complete the sentence.

Ⓐ she
Ⓑ its
Ⓒ their
Ⓓ her

Question Number: 6

The dancers practice every night in order to learn _____ dance steps.

Choose the correct pronoun to complete the sentence.

Ⓐ its
Ⓑ them
Ⓒ their
Ⓓ our

Question Number: 7

Kelly and I have been going to dances for two years now, but her little sister wants to come with us this time. This is _____ first time at a school dance.

Choose the appropriate pronoun.

Ⓐ her
Ⓑ my
Ⓒ she
Ⓓ it

Question Number: 8

_____ went hiking in the mountains together.

Complete the sentence with the appropriate pronoun.

Ⓐ **His**
Ⓑ **Her**
Ⓒ **They**
Ⓓ **Them**

Question Number: 9

I baked fancy Christmas cupcakes for my teacher. She is my favorite teacher and I couldn't wait until Monday to give them to _____.

Choose the correct pronoun.

Ⓐ **she**
Ⓑ **him**
Ⓒ **he**
Ⓓ **her**

Question Number: 10

Alice and Jennifer like going ice skating. _____ are going to the ice skating rink this afternoon.

Choose the correct pronoun.

Ⓐ **their**
Ⓑ **they**
Ⓒ **them**
Ⓓ **her**

Progressive Verb Tense (L.4.1.B)

Question Number: 1

Efrain, accompanied by his parents, _____ to Europe this summer.
Choose the correct progressive verb tense.

Ⓐ are traveling
Ⓑ will be traveling
Ⓒ was traveling
Ⓓ is traveling

Question Number: 2

Darrel and I _____ the football game with friends this Friday night.
Choose the correct verb to complete the sentence.

Ⓐ are attending
Ⓑ am attending
Ⓒ Was attending
Ⓓ will attend

Question Number: 3

Choose the sentence that has the proper progressive verb tense.

Ⓐ **Minnie, Jill, and Sandra are singing the birthday song to Ann right now.**
Ⓑ **Bob, Jim, and Harry have played baseball next summer.**
Ⓒ **One of my five hamsters is getting out of the cage tomorrow night.**
Ⓓ **Twenty-five dollars are too much to charge for that bracelet.**

Question Number: 4

Choose the sentence that has proper verb tense.

Ⓐ **Everyone in my neighborhood, including the woman with nine dogs, were walking each night after dinner.**
Ⓑ **Contestants from Europe, America, and Germany are competing in last year's contest.**
Ⓒ **Neither of the girls is planning to audition for the school play.**
Ⓓ **No one in my history class wish that we had more homework each night.**

Question Number: 5

Jenny, one of my many friends, _____ to buy a new car this summer with money she earns during this school year at her babysitting job.
Choose the correct one.

Ⓐ **Will be saving**
Ⓑ **is saving**
Ⓒ **am saving**
Ⓓ **be hoping**

Question Number: 6

The cheerleader, who was cheering for her team, wore one of the team's new uniforms.**What should the correct sentence be?**

Ⓐ **The cheerleader, who was cheering for her team, were dressed in one of the team's new uniforms.**
Ⓑ **The cheerleader, who was cheering for her team, was wearing one of the team's new uniforms.**
Ⓒ **The cheerleader, who were cheering for her team, were wearing one of the team's new uniforms.**
Ⓓ **The cheerleaders, who was cheering for her teams, will be wearing one of the teams new uniforms.**

Question Number: 7

The trees that keeps waved in the wind on the side of the street show how forceful the wind is.

What should the correct sentence be?

Ⓐ **The trees that waved in the wind on the side of the street show how forceful the wind is.**
Ⓑ **The trees that will be waving in the wind on the side of the street show how forceful the wind is.**
Ⓒ **The trees that keep waving in the wind on the side of the street show how forceful the wind is.**
Ⓓ **The trees that keep waving in the wind on the side of the street shows how forceful the wind is.**

Question Number: 8

The world change so rapidly that we can hardly keep up.
Choose the correct sentence.

- Ⓐ The world will be changing so rapidly that we can hardly keep up.
- Ⓑ The world change so rapidly that we can hardly keep up.
- Ⓒ The world is changing so rapidly that we can hardly keep up.
- Ⓓ The worlds change so rapidly that we can hardly keep up.

Question Number: 9

She sitted at the table by the window when the waiter approached.
Choose the correct sentence.

- Ⓐ She sitting at the table by the window.
- Ⓑ She was sitting at the table by the window.
- Ⓒ She is sitting at the table by the window.
- Ⓓ Shes will be sitting at the table by the window.

Question Number: 10

Kenji and Briana _____ at recess when their parents pick them up for their doctor appointments.
Which verb best completes the sentence?

- Ⓐ play
- Ⓑ will play
- Ⓒ will be playing
- Ⓓ were playing

Modal Auxiliary Verbs (L.4.1.C)

Question Number: 1

(1) Rae and her mother need to find a birthday gift for Rae's father, Joseph. (2) They discussed shopping online, walking to the store in their neighborhood, or going to the mall to find the gift. (3) Because Rae's mother suffers from arthritis, I don't think they will walk to the store to buy the gift. (4) They may decide it's most efficient to buy the gift online.

Which sentence contains an auxiliary verb?

Ⓐ sentence 1
Ⓑ sentences 2 and 3
Ⓒ sentence 4
Ⓓ sentences 3 and 4

Question Number: 2

Oliver may go to school tomorrow if his fever has dissipated.

What is the purpose of the modal auxiliary verb, "may," in the sentence?.

Ⓐ **It is being used to express doubt.**
Ⓑ **It is being used to talk about a future event with uncertainty.**
Ⓒ **It is being used to talk about something that will definitely happen.**
Ⓓ **It is being used to talk about something that definitely will not happen.**

Question Number: 3

Liam can have taken the test before he went on vacation, but he did not inform his teacher about the trip in advance.

Replace "can" with the correct verb in the sentence.

Ⓐ **Will**
Ⓑ **Must**
Ⓒ **Can't**
Ⓓ **Could**

Question Number: 4

Dana had to leave the party when her mother called to inform her of an emergency at home.

What is the auxiliary modal verb in the sentence?

Ⓐ she
Ⓑ at
Ⓒ had
Ⓓ will

Question Number: 5

Choose the sentence that contains a modal auxiliary verb.

Ⓐ You shouldn't have handled your disagreement with physical violence.
Ⓑ I want to have a birthday party.
Ⓒ Everyone needs to look up.
Ⓓ That is the most beautiful painting I have ever seen.

Question Number: 6

Choose the sentence that contains a modal auxiliary verb.

Ⓐ You are a very good reader.
Ⓑ Sara is having a great time on her Hawaiian vacation.
Ⓒ I am not a big fan of Justin Beiber.
Ⓓ You could be a really good student if you applied yourself to your studies.

Question Number: 7

Choose the sentence that contains a modal auxiliary verb.

Ⓐ Jerome has potential to be an excellent science fiction writer.
Ⓑ Margaret is the most beautiful dancer on the stage.
Ⓒ I shall never think another bad thought again.
Ⓓ None of the above

Question Number: 8

(1)If I could dine with any person, living or dead, I would choose Maya Angelou. (2)She endured hardships in her life but went on to become one of the most influential literary figures of the 20th century. (3)I will ask her what inspired her most.
"Will" is not the best verb choice in the 3rd sentence.

What word should the speaker have used instead to express possibility rather than certainty?

Ⓐ can
Ⓑ may
Ⓒ shall
Ⓓ would

Question Number: 9

"Can you hand me that apple?" Marvin asked his mother.
"Yes," she answered. But she didn't move a muscle.

Why did Marvin's mother respond this way?

Ⓐ She had had an extremely long and tiring day at work. Marvin's mother did not want to hand him the apple.
Ⓑ Marvin's mother recognizes she can hand him the apple and knows there is a better way for him to ask using the word "will".
Ⓒ Marvin's mother does not approve of apples.
Ⓓ She thinks Marvin should have to get his own apple.

Question Number: 10

Choose the sentence that correctly uses a modal auxiliary verb.

Ⓐ I might have to see a doctor if this headache does not go away.
Ⓑ I shall all the items on the menu.
Ⓒ She musted remembered to lock the front door before leaving for work each day.
Ⓓ All of the above

Adjectives and Adverbs (L.4.1.D)

Question Number: 1

(1) Mary went to visit her grandmother last weekend. (2) She likes to visit her grand-mother beautiful frequently. (3) While visiting, they enjoy walking. (4) They strolled in the beautiful park and talked. (5) Mary and her grandmother enjoyed their visit.

Identify the _adverb_ used in <u>sentence 2</u>.

Ⓐ likes
Ⓑ visits
Ⓒ frequently
Ⓓ her

Question Number: 2

(1) Mary went to visit her grandmother last weekend. (2) She likes to visit her grandmother frequently. (3) While visiting, they enjoy walking. (4) They strolled in the beautiful park and talked. (5) Mary and her grandmother enjoyed their visit.
Identify the _adjective_ used in <u>sentence 4</u>.

Ⓐ strolled
Ⓑ beautiful
Ⓒ park
Ⓓ talked

Question Number: 3

Zelda and her family visited the Jackson Zoo last weekend although it was alarmingly cold and rainy.

Identify an _adjective_ in the above sentence.

Ⓐ last
Ⓑ although
Ⓒ and
Ⓓ cold

Question Number: 4

Zelda and her family visited the Jackson Zoo last weekend although it was alarmingly cold and rainy.

What is the correct order of words in the sentence?

Ⓐ **Zelda and her family visited the Jackson Zoo last weekend although it was cold alarmingly and rainy.**
Ⓑ **Zelda and her family visited the Jackson Zoo last weekend although it was alarmingly cold and rainy.**
Ⓒ **Zelda and her family visited the Jackson Zoo last weekend although it was rainy and cold.**
Ⓓ **Zelda and her family visited the Jackson Zoo last weekend although it was cold, rainy, and alarmingly.**

Question Number: 5

It was determined that James was the _____ runner on our track team.

Choose the correct adjective to complete the above sentence.

Ⓐ **most fast**
Ⓑ **fastest**
Ⓒ **most fastest**
Ⓓ **faster**

Question Number: 6

(1) Lindsay, Laine, and John were excited. (2) Each put their things in his or her overnight bag. (3) They were going to spend two nights with Aunt Margaret, and the next night with their Auntie Jo.

What is the adjective in sentence 1?

Ⓐ **John**
Ⓑ **Lindsay**
Ⓒ **Laine**
Ⓓ **excited**

Question Number: 7

I think that my daughter is the _____ girl in the world.

Choose the appropriate word for the sentence above.

Ⓐ beautifulest
Ⓑ beautifuler
Ⓒ most beautiful
Ⓓ more beautiful

Question Number: 8

The wind was much _____ than it was last weekend.

Choose the correct _comparative adjective_ to complete the above sentence.

Ⓐ cold
Ⓑ coldest
Ⓒ more cold
Ⓓ colder

Question Number: 9

While standing at the intersection, I heard a loud noise and turned my head to see the _____ wreck imaginable.

Choose the proper comparative adjective to complete the above sentence.

Ⓐ horrificest
Ⓑ most horrificest
Ⓒ more horrificest
Ⓓ most horrific

Question Number: 10

The huge tiger hungrily stealthily walked in the black, spiky bush getting ready to pounce.

What's the correct order of adverbs in the sentence above?

Ⓐ Huge, spiky
Ⓑ Hungrily and stealthily
Ⓒ Stealthily and hungrily
Ⓓ Black spiky

Prepositional Phrases (L.4.1.E)

Question Number: 1

Choose the sentence that contains a prepositional phrase.

- Ⓐ The monkey was washing its paws.
- Ⓑ The lion jumped into the pool of cool water.
- Ⓒ That is the most beautiful dog I have ever seen.
- Ⓓ When you decide, let me know.

Question Number: 2

You will find the new notebooks underneath the journals.
Identify the *prepositional phrase* in the above sentence.

- Ⓐ will find
- Ⓑ notebooks underneath
- Ⓒ new notebooks
- Ⓓ underneath the journals

Question Number: 3

Choose the sentence that contains a prepositional phrase.

- Ⓐ Please put your paper down so that others won't see your answers.
- Ⓑ Because he doesn't have enough money to buy ice cream, he must do without.
- Ⓒ Do not leave for school without your lunch box.
- Ⓓ Please don't forget to let the dog in.

Question Number: 4

Choose the sentence that contains a prepositional phrase.

- Ⓐ When entering the room, Ana tripped on the rug and fell.
- Ⓑ I want to see the Rocky Mountains.
- Ⓒ Everyone needs to look up.
- Ⓓ That is the most beautiful painting I have ever seen.

Question Number: 5

Finding his money, Lee and Jose rushed to join their friends at the fair.

Identify the prepositional phrase in the above sentence.

- Ⓐ finding his money
- Ⓑ rushed to join
- Ⓒ their friends
- Ⓓ at the fair

Question Number: 6

Identify the sentence that contains two prepositional phrases.

Ⓐ Terrance went into the room to get his book.
Ⓑ Terrance went into the room.
Ⓒ Terrance went into the room and sat in his favorite chair.
Ⓓ Terrance sat in his favorite chair to read.

Question Number: 7

The puppy barked loudly and chased the kitten across the yard.
Identify the prepositional phrase in the above sentence.

Ⓐ barked loudly
Ⓑ chased across
Ⓒ barked loudly and chased
Ⓓ across the yard

Question Number: 8

Identify the sentence that contains a prepositional phrase.

Ⓐ The intoxicating aroma filled the air.
Ⓑ The aroma coming from the kitchen was inviting.
Ⓒ I forgot to purchase a loaf of bread.
Ⓓ A lovely young woman watched as the band marched.

Question Number: 9

Identify the sentence that DOES NOT contains a prepositional phrase.

Ⓐ Are you going to let him answer the question?
Ⓑ The answer to the question was wrong.
Ⓒ The teacher put a huge red checkmark on my paper.
Ⓓ The questions on this test were very difficult.

Question Number: 10

The fox chased the deer down the trail.
Identify the prepositional phrase in the sentence above.

Ⓐ chased the deer
Ⓑ the fox
Ⓒ down the trail
Ⓓ the deer down

Complete Sentences (L.4.1.F)

Question Number: 1

Jordan wants to go outside and play with her neighbor her mother said she had to clean up her room first.
Which answer choice corrects this run-on sentence?

Ⓐ **Jordan wants to go outside and play with her neighbor, but her mother said she had to clean up her room first.**
Ⓑ **Jordan wants to go outside and play but her mother won't let her.**
Ⓒ **Jordan wants, to go outside and play with her neighbor but her nother said she had to clean up her room first.**
Ⓓ **Jordan wants to go outside. And play with her neighbor. But her mother said she had to clean up her room first.**

Question Number: 2

George Washington Carver is best known for his work with peanuts but he also taught his students about crop rotation that's when farmers plant different crops each year to avoid draining the soil of its nutrients.
Which answer choice corrects the run-on sentence above?

Ⓐ **George Washington Carver is best known for his work with peanuts, but he also taught his students about crop rotation, that's when farmers plant different crops each year to avoid draining the soil of its nutrients**

Ⓑ **George Washington Carver is best known for his work with peanuts, but he also taught his students about crop rotation. That's when farmers plant different crops each year to avoid draining the soil of its nutrients.**

Ⓒ **George Washington Carver is best known for his work with peanuts. But he also taught his students about crop rotation. That's when farmers plant different crops each year to avoid draining the soil of its nutrients**

Ⓓ **George Washington Carver is best known for his work with peanuts but he also taught his students about crop rotation that's when farmers plant different crops each year to avoid draining the soil of its nutrients**

Question Number: 3

Which answer choice is a fragment, rather than a complete sentence?

Ⓐ **Be careful what you wish for.**
Ⓑ **He should not run with scissors.**
Ⓒ **If you can't say something nice.**
Ⓓ **Don't say anything at all.**

Question Number: 4

Three ways to transfer heat.
What would transform this fragment into a complete sentence?

Ⓐ **Replacing the period with a question mark at the end of the sentence**
Ⓑ **Adding "convection, conduction, and radiation" to the end of the sentence.**
Ⓒ **Adding "There are" to the beginning of the sentence.**
Ⓓ **Nothing. The sentence is complete already.**

Question Number: 5

(1)Producers make their own food from the sun during a process called photosynthesis. (2)The Greek root, "photo," means "light." (3)Means "to put together." (4)So "photosynthesis" means "to put together with light," which is exactly what plants do when they make their own food.
Which sentence is a fragment, rather than a complete sentence?

Ⓐ **Sentence 1**
Ⓑ **Sentence 2**
Ⓒ **Sentence 3**
Ⓓ **Sentence 4**

Question Number: 6

(1)Jawaad held his head high. (2)As he strode to the front of the classroom to present his research report. (3)The report compared the Norse god, Thor, to the Marvel Comic version of Thor. (4)He was proud of his work and thought the class would really enjoy it.
Choose the best edited version of the above paragraph. Pay attention to run-on sentences and fragments.

Ⓐ **Jawaad held his head high. As he strode to the front of the classroom to present his research report. The report compared the Norse god, Thor, to the Marvel Comic version of Thor. He was proud of the work and thought the class would really enjoyed it.**

Ⓑ **Jawaad held his head high. As he strode to the front of the classroom to present his research report, the report compared the Norse god, Thor, to the Marvel Comic version of Thor. He was proud of the work and thought the class would really enjoyed it.**

Ⓒ **Jawaad held his head high. As he strode to the front of the classroom to present his research report. The report compared the Norse god, Thor, to the Marvel Comic version of Thor he was proud of the work and thought the class would really enjoyed it.**

Ⓓ **Jawaad held his head high as he strode to the front of the classroom to present his research report. The report compared the Norse god, Thor, to the Marvel Comic version of Thor. He was proud of the work and thought the class would really enjoyed it.**

Question Number: 7

Choose the run-on sentence.

Ⓐ Felix has a mischievous spirit he is somehow quite well-behaved.
Ⓑ Margaret is the most beautiful dancer on the stage.
Ⓒ The sky was the limit for a bright, energetic, young prodigy like Ben.
Ⓓ None of the above

Question Number: 8

(1)If I could dine with any person, living or dead, I would choose Maya Angelou. (2)She endured hardships in her life but went on to become one of the most influential literary figures of the 20th century. (3)I would ask her what inspired her most.
Identify the run-on sentence.

Ⓐ Sentence 1
Ⓑ Sentence 2
Ⓒ Sentence 3
Ⓓ None of the above

Question Number: 9

A really great pair of shoes.
What would transform the fragment into a complete sentence?

Ⓐ A really great pair of shoes, two ironed shirts, and two pairs of dress pants.
Ⓑ A really great pair of shoes should be both stylish and comfortable.
Ⓒ Doesn't need a really great pair of shoes.
Ⓓ All of the above.

Question Number: 10

Choose the complete sentence.

Ⓐ While she is a very sweet puppy, I can't justify adopting her.
Ⓑ While she is a very sweet puppy.
Ⓒ Because my apartment is too small.
Ⓓ I can't justify adopting this puppy my apartment is too small.

Frequently Confused Words (L.4.1.G)

Question Number: 1

Divya and her family celebrate Diwali, a traditional festival in _____ culture.
Choose the correct word to complete the sentence.

Ⓐ their
Ⓑ they're
Ⓒ there
Ⓓ None of the above.

Question Number: 2

Place your projects over _____ until it's time to present.
Choose the correct word to complete the sentence.

Ⓐ their
Ⓑ they're
Ⓒ there
Ⓓ None of the above

Question Number: 3

Gretchen and Laura are thankful _____ able to peer edit each other's writing.
Choose the correct word to complete the sentence.

Ⓐ their
Ⓑ they're.
Ⓒ there
Ⓓ None of the above

Question Number: 4

We're going too my grandmother's house for Thanksgiving, but we'll be driving back home on Friday.
Choose the best edited version of the sentence.

Ⓐ We're going two my grandmother's house for Thanksgiving, but we'll be driving back home on Friday.
Ⓑ Were going too my grandmother's house for Thanksgiving, but we'll be driving back home on Friday.
Ⓒ We're going to my grandmother's house for Thanksgiving, but we'll be driving back home on Friday.
Ⓓ The sentence is correct already.

Question Number: 5

I assumed the mall would be crowded today. Were are all the people?
What error did the writer make?

Ⓐ She wrote a run-on sentence.
Ⓑ She spelled "assumed" incorrectly.
Ⓒ She used "were" instead of "where."
Ⓓ She wrote a fragment.

Question Number: 6

We don't have any milk or bread, so _____ going to the grocery store right this instant.
Which word best completes the sentence?

Ⓐ were
Ⓑ we're
Ⓒ where
Ⓓ there

Question Number: 7

I can't take another breathe until I know how this book will end.
What error did the writer make?

Ⓐ She should have used the word, "breath," rather than "breathe."
Ⓑ She should never hold her breath because she could faint.
Ⓒ She should have used "took," rather than "take."
Ⓓ She should have used "an other" instead of "another."

Question Number: 8

Amal _____ his exam with flying colors. He knew it was because he studied so hard.
Choose the correct word to complete the sentence.

Ⓐ pessed
Ⓑ pest
Ⓒ past
Ⓓ passed

Question Number: 9

I have to _____ that science does not come easily for me. If I want to do well I will have to work at it.

Choose the correct word to complete the sentence.

Ⓐ except
Ⓑ accept
Ⓒ expect
Ⓓ none of the above

Question Number: 10

Choose the correct sentence.

Ⓐ We base our school rules around the common principal that everyone should be treated with respect.
Ⓑ The principal called Evelyn to her office to reward her for perfect attendance.
Ⓒ Jamar was extatic when he was chosen as a principle dancer in the ballet.
Ⓓ All of the above

How is it Capitalized? (L.4.2.A)

Question Number: 1

Although spring and summer are my favorite seasons, our family gathering on thanksgiving makes november my favorite month.
Identify the words that need to be capitalized in the above sentence.

Ⓐ **Spring, November**
Ⓑ **Thanksgiving, November**
Ⓒ **Summer, Thanksgiving**
Ⓓ **Seasons, November**

Question Number: 2

<u>dr. j. howard smith</u>
1141 east palm street
washington, la 98654
Correctly capitalize the underlined portion of the above address.

Ⓐ **Dr. J. Howard Smith**
Ⓑ **DR. J. Howard Smith**
Ⓒ **Dr. J. howard smith**
Ⓓ **Dr. j. Howard Smith**

Question Number: 3

dr. j. howard smith
<u>1141 east palm street</u>
washington, la 98654
Correctly capitalize the underlined portion of the above address.

Ⓐ **1141 east Palm Street**
Ⓑ **1141 East palm Street**
Ⓒ **1141 east palm Street**
Ⓓ **1141 East Palm Street**

Question Number: 4

dr. j. howard smith
1141 east palm street
<u>washington, la 98654</u>
Correctly capitalize the underlined portion of the above address.

Ⓐ **Washington, LA 98654**
Ⓑ **Washington, La 98654**
Ⓒ **washington, LA 98654**
Ⓓ **washington, La 98654**

Question Number: 5

Next Semester, I plan to take English, History, Math, Spanish, and Music.

Edit the above sentence for capitalization. Choose the sentence that is written correctly.

Ⓐ Next Semester, I plan to take English, History, Spanish, and music.
Ⓑ Next semester, I plan to take English, History, Spanish, and Music.
Ⓒ Next semester, I plan to take english, history, spanish, and music.
Ⓓ Next semester, I plan to take English, history, Spanish, and music.

Question Number: 6

In Mrs. Hart's English class, we are reading <u>the indian in the cupboard</u>.

Choose the title of the book that has correct capitalization.

Ⓐ <u>The Indian In The Cupboard</u>
Ⓑ <u>The Indian in the Cupboard</u>
Ⓒ <u>The indian in the Cupboard</u>
Ⓓ <u>the Indian in the Cupboard</u>

Question Number: 7

The entire family is excited and looking forward to our visit with aunt jenny, my uncle, my grand-father, and grandma.

Choose the correctly capitalized version of the above sentence.

Ⓐ The entire Family is excited and looking forward to our visit with Aunt jenny, my uncle, my grandfather, and Grandma.
Ⓑ The entire family is excited and looking forward to our visit with Aunt jenny, my uncle, my Grandfather, and Grandma.
Ⓒ The entire family is excited and looking forward to our visit with Aunt Jenny, my uncle, my grandfather, and Grandma.
Ⓓ The entire family is excited and looking forward to our visit with aunt Jenny, my Uncle, my Grandfather, and Grandma.

Question Number: 8

yours truly,
timmy newlin

Choose correctly capitalized version of the above letter closing.

Ⓐ **Yours Truly,**
Timmy Newlin

Ⓑ **yours truly,**
Timmy Newlin

Ⓒ **Yours truly,**
Timmy Newlin

Ⓓ **Yours truly,**
Timmy newlin

Question Number: 9

the chicago river runs into the mississippi valley waterways.

Which words should be capitalized?

Ⓐ **The, Chicago**
Ⓑ **The, Chicago River**
Ⓒ **The, Chicago River, Mississippi**
Ⓓ **The, Chicago River, Mississippi Valley**

Question Number: 10

I love these lime green nike shoes that my grandma got me for my birthday.

Which word in the above sentence should be capitalized?

Ⓐ **grandma**
Ⓑ **birthday**
Ⓒ **nike**
Ⓓ **shoes**

What's the Punctuation? (L.4.2.B/C)

Question Number: 1

Choose the sentence that is punctuated correctly.

Ⓐ Before I go to bed each night I brush my teeth.
Ⓑ The rabbit scampered across the yard, and ran into the woods.
Ⓒ I don't like to watch scary movies but I like to read scary books.
Ⓓ Our teacher gave us time to study before she gave us the test.

Question Number: 2

Choose the sentence that correctly punctuates a quotation.

Ⓐ "Did you remember to lock the door," asked Jenny?
Ⓑ "Did you remember to lock the door? asked Jenny."
Ⓒ Jenny asked "Did you remember to lock the door?"
Ⓓ Jenny asked, "Did you remember to lock the door?"

Question Number: 3

Choose the sentence that contains a punctuation error.

Ⓐ Cindy wants to go to the mall this afternoon, but her mother will not let her.
Ⓑ Wendy stayed up all night completing her science project, but forgot to take it with her.
Ⓒ Henry forgot to close the gate securely, so his dog escaped from the backyard.
Ⓓ Jimmy and John joined the Army; Billy and George joined the Navy.

Question Number: 4

Do you know Shel Silverstein's poem The Boa Constrictor our teacher asked.

What is the correct way to write the sentence above?

Ⓐ "Do you know Shel Silverstein's poem 'The Boa Constrictor'?" our teacher asked.
Ⓑ "Do you know Shel Silverstein's poem "The Boa Constrictor"? our teacher asked.
Ⓒ "Do you know Shel Silverstein's poem The Boa Constrictor"? our teacher asked.
Ⓓ "Do you know Shel Silverstein's poem The Boa Constrictor" she asked?

Question Number: 5

Of all the poems in his latest book she said this is my favorite. It's really very funny she added.

What is the correct way to write the sentence above?

Ⓐ "Of all the poems in his latest book" she said "this is my favorite." "It's really very funny she added."

Ⓑ "Of all the poems in his latest book," she said, "this is my favorite. It's really very funny," she added.

Ⓒ "Of all the poems in his latest book she said this is my favorite. It's really very funny she added."

Ⓓ "Of all the poems in his latest book," she said "this is my favorite. "It's really very funny" she added.

Question Number: 6

Tom's English professor asked him what was wrong.

What is the correct way to write the sentence above?

Ⓐ The sentence is correct.

Ⓑ Tom's English professor asked him "what was wrong?"

Ⓒ "Tom's English professor asked him what was wrong."

Ⓓ Tom's English professor, asked him, what was wrong.

Question Number: 7

Choose the sentence that is punctuated correctly.

Ⓐ Machiavelli's <u>The Prince</u> begins, "All states, all powers, that have held and hold rule over men have been and are either republics or principalities." [public domain text]

Ⓑ machiavelli's <u>The Prince</u> begins, All states, all powers, that have held and hold rule over men have been and are either republics or principalities.

Ⓒ Machiavelli's <u>The Prince</u> begins "All states, all powers, that have held and hold rule over men have been and are either republics or principalities."

Ⓓ Machiavelli's <u>The Prince</u> begins all states, all powers, that have held and hold rule over men have been and are either republics or principalities.

Question Number: 8

Choose the sentence that is punctuated correctly. [from Peter Pan- public domain]

Ⓐ J.M. Barrie wrote all children, except one, grow up.
Ⓑ J.M. Barrie wrote, All children, except one, grow up.
Ⓒ J.M. Barrie wrote, "All children, except one, grow up."
Ⓓ J.M. Barrie wrote "All children, except one, grow up"

Question Number: 9

Choose the sentence that is punctuated correctly.

Ⓐ In his book, *Peter Pan*, J.M. Barrie says Wendy, knew that she must grow up.
Ⓑ In his book, *Peter Pan*, J.M. Barrie says Wendy "knew that she must grow up."
Ⓒ In his book, *Peter Pan*, J.M. Barrie says wendy, "knew that she must grow up
Ⓓ In his book, *Peter Pan*, J.M. Barrie says Wendy, "knew that she must grow up."

Question Number: 10

Choose the sentence that is punctuated correctly.

Ⓐ The snake was long black and scaly.
Ⓑ The snake slithered across the kitchen floor and Tiffany ran to her bedroom to get away.
Ⓒ I don't like to watch scary movies but I like to read scary books.
Ⓓ The snake slithered across the kitchen floor, and Tiffany ran to her bedroom to get away.

How is it Spelled? (L.4.2.D)

Question Number: 1

Vargas asked his partner, "Could you please _____ your question to make it easier to understand?"
Choose the correctly spelled work that best completes the sentence.

Ⓐ clearify
Ⓑ Clerify
Ⓒ carefully
Ⓓ clarify

Question Number: 2

Find the misspelled word.

Ⓐ ostrich
Ⓑ vehicel
Ⓒ wings
Ⓓ horse

Question Number: 3

Which of the following words are spelled correctly?

Ⓐ Pollution
Ⓑ Polution
Ⓒ Plloution
Ⓓ Polltion

Question Number: 4

Mom asked the mayor, "Do you beleive in ghosts?"
Choose the word that is incorrectly spelled in the above sentence.

Ⓐ asked
Ⓑ mayor
Ⓒ beleive
Ⓓ ghosts

Question Number: 5

Choose the word that is correctly spelled.

Ⓐ monkies
Ⓑ strawberrys
Ⓒ cherrys
Ⓓ donkeys

Question Number: 6

Nicky set the table for dinner, but she forgot to place knifes at each place setting.
Choose that word that is incorrectly spelled in the above sentence.

Ⓐ dinner
Ⓑ knifes
Ⓒ setting
Ⓓ table

Question Number: 7

Choose the word that is NOT spelled correctly.

Ⓐ Collaterol
Ⓑ Enthusiasm
Ⓒ Infrequently
Ⓓ Vigorous

Question Number: 8

Choose the sentence with the misspelled word.

Ⓐ Rosemary skipped across the room to give her grandfather a hug.
Ⓑ I bought a beautiful new aquarium for my goldfish while at the flea market.
Ⓒ After tripping in the cafeteria and spilling her tray, Mary ran from the room crying.
Ⓓ When I opened the box, I realized that the attachment I wanted was sold seperately and not included in the package.

Question Number: 9

Choose the sentence that contains a misspelled word.

Ⓐ Our class just completed a study on the lifecycle of butterflies.
Ⓑ The delivery man stacked the packages and boxxes in his truck.
Ⓒ The turtle jumped from its log, creating quite a splash.
Ⓓ When firefighters were able to contain the flames, the crowd cheered.

Question Number: 10

Which word below is spelled correctly?

Ⓐ nerrate
Ⓑ nihrayt
Ⓒ narrete
Ⓓ narrate

Word Choice: Attending to Precision (L.4.3.A)

Question Number: 1

Alexander _____ into the living room to show off his new suit. He had a very high opinion of himself!
Choose the word that best completes the sentence.

Ⓐ **walked**
Ⓑ **strutted**
Ⓒ **trudged**
Ⓓ **waddled**

Question Number: 2

Collecting the garbage was _____ work, but Tom was happy to do it. The job wore on his body, especially during the hottest days of summer, but he knew he was providing an important public service to his community.
Choose the word that best completes the sentence.

Ⓐ **uncomfortable**
Ⓑ **grueling**
Ⓒ **bad**
Ⓓ **stupid**

Question Number: 3

Dante was _____ about his award for most improved swimmer. He had never wanted any-thing more!
Choose the word that best completes sentence.

Ⓐ **peaceful**
Ⓑ **happy**
Ⓒ **elated**
Ⓓ **disappointed**

Question Number: 4

The baby babbled sweetly, making it difficult for her mother to be upset about the _____ mess she had made when she threw spaghetti all over the kitchen.
Choose the word that best completes the sentence.

Ⓐ **gigantic**
Ⓑ **big**
Ⓒ **wide**
Ⓓ **deep**

Question Number: 5

The defendant's fingerprint at the scene of the crime was the most _____ evidence in the trial. The jury had no choice but to convict her.
Choose the word that best completes the sentence.

(A) worst
(B) damaging
(C) bad
(D) wonderful

Question Number: 6

Shelby was a _____. She was fiesty, and she did not let anyone push her around.
Choose the word that best completes the sentence.

(A) ham
(B) scrooge
(C) shrinking violet
(D) fireball

Question Number: 7

The girls _____ to the front of the crowd to get a glimpse of their favorite boy band.
Choose the word that best completes the sentence.

(A) walked
(B) skipped
(C) dove
(D) clambered

Question Number: 8

Anne is paying attention to choosing precise words in her writing. Which sentence should she use in her personal narrative to describe the overflowing bathtub?

(A) The water <u>dripping</u> over the edge reminded her of a waterfall.
(B) The water <u>spraying</u> over the edge reminded her of a waterfall.
(C) The water <u>bubbling</u> over the edge reminded her of a waterfall.
(D) The water <u>cascading</u> over the edge reminded her of a waterfall.

Question Number: 9

Riley is paying attention to choosing precise words in his writing. Which sentence should he use to help persuade the reader to recycle?

Ⓐ Recycling <u>cuts down on</u> the amount of waste that goes into landfills each year.
Ⓑ Recycling <u>helps us put a little bit less</u> waste into landfills each year.
Ⓒ Recycling <u>reduces</u> the amount of waste that goes into landfills each year.
Ⓓ Recycling <u>makes us put not as much</u> waste into landfills each year.

Question Number: 10

Janet _____ with delight when she called her mother to say she had been accepted to her top choice college.
Choose the word that best completes the sentence.

Ⓐ squealed
Ⓑ spoke
Ⓒ sneezed
Ⓓ growled

Punctuating for Effect! (L.4.3.B)

Question Number: 1

Jermaine mother said you have to clean your room.
Choose the puntuation that means Jermain's mother is speaking to him.

Ⓐ   Jermaine mother said you have to clean your room.
Ⓑ   "Jermaine, Mother said you have to clean your room."
Ⓒ   Jermaine Mother said, "You have to clean your room."
Ⓓ   "Jermaine," Mother said, "you have to clean your room."

Question Number: 2

Jermaine mother said you have to clean your room.
Choose the puntuation that means a third character is shouting at Jermaine to tell him his mother said to clean his room.

Ⓐ   "Jermaine," Mother said, "you have to clean your room!"
Ⓑ   "Jermaine, Mother said you have to clean your room!"
Ⓒ   "Jermaine," Mother said, "you have to clean your room?"
Ⓓ   "Jermaine, Mother said you have to clean your room."

Question Number: 3

Dante was elated about his award for most improved swimmer. He had never wanted anything more
Choose the most appropriate end punctuation.

Ⓐ   .
Ⓑ   ?
Ⓒ   !
Ⓓ $

Question Number: 4

Choose the sentence that is punctuated correctly.

Ⓐ   The tiger crept carefully through the jungle?
Ⓑ   The tiger crept carefully through the jungle!
Ⓒ   The tiger crept carefully through the jungle
Ⓓ   The tiger crept carefully through the jungle.

Question Number: 5

James was furious when Gemma squirted ketchup all over his new white shirt(1) Sheesh (2) What did Gemma expect to happen (3)
Choose the appropriate end punctuation for sentence 1.

Ⓐ .
Ⓑ !
Ⓒ ?
Ⓓ *

Question Number: 6

James was furious when Gemma squirted ketchup all over his new white shirt(1) Sheesh (2) What did Gemma expect to happen (3)
Choose the appropriate end punctuation for sentence 2.

Ⓐ .
Ⓑ !
Ⓒ ?
Ⓓ *

Question Number: 7

James was furious when Gemma squirted ketchup all over his new white shirt(1) Sheesh (2) What did Gemma expect to happen (3)
Choose the appropriate end punctuation for sentence 3.

Ⓐ .
Ⓑ !
Ⓒ ?
Ⓓ *

Question Number: 8

Wow( ) I can't believe I am going to compete in the national chess competition for my age group!

Which punctuation best follows "Wow"?

Ⓐ .
Ⓑ !
Ⓒ ?
Ⓓ &

Question Number: 9

Which of the following sentences is NOT punctuated correctly?

Ⓐ Gee whiz!
Ⓑ I can't believe my good fortune!
Ⓒ Why does water evaporate faster when the sun is out!
Ⓓ Clean your room this instant!

Question Number: 10

Which of the following sentences is punctuated correctly?

Ⓐ She startled me when she jumped out of the bushes!
Ⓑ I'm so hungry I'm afraid I won't make it to lunch?
Ⓒ Our teacher is an amazing #storyteller
Ⓓ None of the above

Finding the Meaning (L.4.3.C)

Question Number: 1

The milk is extracted from the coconut, which is used to prepare a variety of dishes and sweets.

What does the word _extracted_ mean in the above sentence?

- Ⓐ **To put in**
- Ⓑ **To take out of something**
- Ⓒ **To make**
- Ⓓ **To throw out**

Question Number: 2

The poor woman was despondent after losing everything she owned in the fire.

Using context clues from the above sentence, the word _despondent_ means:

- Ⓐ **excited**
- Ⓑ **questioning**
- Ⓒ **despairing**
- Ⓓ **radiant**

Question Number: 3

My father tried to console me after my dog died, but nothing he did made me feel better.

Based on the above sentence, console means:

- Ⓐ **entertain**
- Ⓑ **comfort**
- Ⓒ **talk to**
- Ⓓ **explain**

Question Number: 4

The sleepy kittens crawled into bed with their mother. They quickly nestled cozily beside her and went to sleep.

The word _nestled_ means:

- Ⓐ **purred softly**
- Ⓑ **lay down**
- Ⓒ **leaned against**
- Ⓓ **snuggled up to**

Question Number: 5

Larry gawked in wide-eyed astonishment at the woman wearing the glass hat with fish swimming in it.
Based on the above sentence, the best meaning for the word _gawked_ is:

Ⓐ glanced at
Ⓑ stared stupidly
Ⓒ laughed at
Ⓓ yelled at

Question Number: 6

If the talking does not cease immediately, you will have 50 additional math problems for home-work.
The word _cease_ means:

Ⓐ become less noisy
Ⓑ continue
Ⓒ decrease
Ⓓ stop

Question Number: 7

The young men rode their bikes 60 miles to the fair. They did not stop for a break the entire trip. Once they arrived, they were too <u>weary</u> to walk around and enjoy the rides, so they simply lounged on the bleachers and watched the quilt judging.
The word weary means:

Ⓐ excited
Ⓑ tired
Ⓒ energized
Ⓓ enthusiastic

Question Number: 8

The young men rode their bikes 60 miles to the fair. They did not stop for a break the entire trip. Once they arrived, they were too weary to walk around and enjoy the ride, so they simply lounged on the bleachers and watched the quilt judging.
The word _lounged_ means:

Ⓐ watched
Ⓑ sat rigidly
Ⓒ stood
Ⓓ relaxed

Question Number: 9

At the football game Friday night, Bill broke his leg when he plummeted to the ground from the top of the bleachers.

Based on the context clues in the above sentence, the best meaning of the word _plummeted_ is:

Ⓐ floated
Ⓑ drifted
Ⓒ slipped
Ⓓ plunged

Question Number: 10

The weather man is predicting several days of frigid temperatures in the mountains. After watching the weather report, I decided to pack thermal shirts and pants, wool sweaters, gloves, and my warmest coat for the camping trip this weekend.

According to the sentence above, the word _frigid_ means:

Ⓐ rising
Ⓑ freezing
Ⓒ warm
Ⓓ chilly

Context Clues (L.4.4.A)

Question Number: 1

Franklin D. Roosevelt gave his first inaugural address in 1933, during the midst of the Great Depression. He famously said, "The only thing we have to fear is... fear itself." His <u>sentiment</u> helped assuage the fears of many Americans, giving them hope for better days ahead.

What is the meaning of the word, "sentiment," in the paragraph above?

Ⓐ **A person who often cries**
Ⓑ **A view or attitude toward a situation or event**
Ⓒ **A nice piece of jewelry**
Ⓓ **Blame**

Question Number: 2

Franklin D. Roosevelt gave his first inaugural address in 1933, during the midst of the Great Depression. He famously said, "The only thing we have to fear is... fear itself." This sentiment helped <u>assuage</u> the fears of many Americans, giving them hope for better days ahead.

What is the meaning of the word, "assuage," in the paragraph above?

Ⓐ **To make worse**
Ⓑ **To ease**
Ⓒ **To heighten**
Ⓓ **To strengthen**

Question Number: 3

The restaurant catered to an <u>affluent</u> crowd. The food was very expensive, the tablecloths were crisp and white, and patrons were expected to dress nicely.

What is the meaning of the word, "affluent," in the paragraph above?

Ⓐ **practical**
Ⓑ **wealthy**
Ⓒ **honest**
Ⓓ **poor**

Question Number: 4

The restaurant catered to an affluent crowd. The food was very expensive, the tablecloths were crisp and white, and <u>patrons</u> were expected to dress nicely in order to eat there.

What is the meaning of the word, "patrons," in the paragraph above?

Ⓐ **Doctors**
Ⓑ **waiters**
Ⓒ **cooks**
Ⓓ **customers**

Question Number: 5

In Charles Dickens's classic tale, Ebenezer Scrooge is a <u>miser</u>-- someone who wishes to spend as little money as possible. As a result, his life is devoid of any meaningful relationships with other people. He does not have any true friends to speak of.

In the paragraph above, what is the meaning of the word, "miser?"

Ⓐ **Someone who gives gifts often**
Ⓑ **Someone who wishes to spend as little money as possible**
Ⓒ **Someone who thinks of others before themselves**
Ⓓ **Someone who is very old**

Question Number: 6

In Charles Dickens's classic tale, Ebenezer Scrooge is a miser-- someone who wishes to spend as little money as possible. As a result, his life is <u>devoid</u> of any meaningful relationships with other people. He does not have any true friends to speak of.

In the paragraph above, what is the meaning of the word, "devoid?"

Ⓐ **Blooming**
Ⓑ **Decorated**
Ⓒ **Filled with**
Ⓓ **Lacking entirely**

Question Number: 7

The hospital <u>corridor</u> was long and cold. Door after door opened into room after room of patients in various stages of rest and recovery. Hazel was earnest in her desire to bring some degree of joy to each of them. That's what clowns are for, after all!

What is the meaning of the word, "corridor," in the paragraph above?

Ⓐ **bed**
Ⓑ **room**
Ⓒ **desk**
Ⓓ **hallway**

Question Number: 8

The hospital corridor was long and cold. Door after door opened into room after room of patients in various stages of rest and recovery. Hazel was <u>earnest</u> in her desire to bring some degree of joy to each of them. That's what clowns are for, after all!

What is the meaning of the word, "earnest," in the paragraph above?

Ⓐ **Willing**
Ⓑ **Excited**
Ⓒ **Money that shows serious intent to do a deal**
Ⓓ **A serious and intent mental state**

Question Number: 9

Marcus decided to <u>invest</u> in Mel and Deena's lemonade stand. He gave them twenty dollars to buy fresh lemons, cups, and sugar. In return Mel and Deena will reimburse him with money they earn selling the lemonade plus ten percent of each cup they sell.

In the paragraph above, what is the meaning of the word, "invest?"

Ⓐ **To really enjoy lemonade**
Ⓑ **To cheer someone one by clapping and shouting**
Ⓒ **To give someone money for fun**
Ⓓ **To give someone money with hopes of making money**

Question Number: 10

Marcus decided to invest in Mel and Deena's lemonade stand. He gave them twenty dollars to buy fresh lemons, cups, and sugar. In return Mel and Deena will <u>reimburse</u> him with money they earn selling the lemonade plus ten percent of each cup they sell.

In the paragraph above, what is the meaning of the word, "reimburse."

Ⓐ **To repay**
Ⓑ **To hit**
Ⓒ **To shower**
Ⓓ **To take**

The Meaning of Words (L.4.4.B)

Question Number: 1

Mindy was surprised to discover how disorganized the students had left the books. What is the meaning of the word <u>disorganized</u>?

Ⓐ organized
Ⓑ Not organized
Ⓒ neat
Ⓓ torn

Question Number: 2

Which of the following words contains a prefix that means <u>again</u>?

Ⓐ preview
Ⓑ international
Ⓒ rewind
Ⓓ disagree

Question Number: 3

Which of the following words refers to half of the globe?

Ⓐ longitude
Ⓑ hemisphere
Ⓒ parallel
Ⓓ latitude

Question Number: 4

The prefix 'sub' in submarine means:

Ⓐ back or again
Ⓑ above or extra
Ⓒ under or below
Ⓓ across or over

Question Number: 5

The prefix 'hyper' in hyperactive means:

Ⓐ within, into
Ⓑ over or excessive
Ⓒ lacking or without
Ⓓ out of or former

Question Number: 6

If biology is the study of life, which answer choice explains the meaning of the word *geology*?

Ⓐ appreciation for the earth
Ⓑ a science class
Ⓒ the study of the earth
Ⓓ the study of life

Question Number: 7

Which of the following does NOT contain an affix?

Ⓐ autograph
Ⓑ photograph
Ⓒ telegraph
Ⓓ graphing

Question Number: 8

Choose the Latin suffix in the word <u>nonlikable</u>.

Ⓐ non
Ⓑ like
Ⓒ kable
Ⓓ able

Question Number: 9

What is the Latin root of the word <u>retractable</u>

Ⓐ re
Ⓑ retract
Ⓒ tract
Ⓓ able

Question Number: 10

Which word contains the Greek root that means 'time'?

Ⓐ chronicle
Ⓑ democracy
Ⓒ metamorphic
Ⓓ phonetics

For Your Reference (L.4.4.C)

Question Number: 1

Where would one look to find the definition of a key word when reading a science text-book?

- Ⓐ the glossary
- Ⓑ the thesaurus
- Ⓒ the dictionary
- Ⓓ the table of contents

Question Number: 2

Component. — N. component; component part, integral part, integrant part[obs3]; element, constituent, ingredient, leaven; part and parcel; contents; appurtenance; feature; member &c. (part) 51; personnel. V. enter into, enter into the composition of; be a component &c. n; be part of, form part of &c. 51; merge in, be merged in; be implicated in; share in &c. (participate) 778; belong to, appertain to; combine, inhere in, unite. form, make, constitute, compose. Adj. forming &c. v. inclusive.

What part of speech is the word, "component," in the thesaurus entry above?

- Ⓐ adjective
- Ⓑ verb
- Ⓒ adverb
- Ⓓ noun

Question Number: 3

Si·lently, *adv.* [f. SILENT *a.* + -LY².]
1. In a silent manner; without speaking, in silence; without noise or commotion, noiselessly, quietly; without mention or notice.
1570-6 LAMBARDE *Peramb. Kent* (1826) 157, I could not silently slip over such impieties. **1590** SHAKS. *Mids. N.* III. i. 206 Tye vp my louers tongue, bring him silently. **1617** MORYSON *Itin.* I. 246 The Turkey company in London was at this time..silently enjoying the safety and profit of this trafficke. **1667** MILTON *P. L.* v. 130 She..silently a gentle tear let fall. **1730** WATERLAND *Rem. Clarke's Exp. Ch. Catech.* ii, What the compilers recommended chiefly to our faith, he silently passes over. **1784** COWPER *Task* IV. 419 These ask with painful shyness, and, refus'd Because deserving, silently retire! **1832** LYTTON *E. Aram* I. xi, Ellinor silently made room for her cousin beside herself. **1878** LECKY *Eng. in 18th C.* I. 313 Most of the..congregations had silently discarded the old doctrine of the Trinity.
†**2.** Gradually, imperceptibly. *Obs.*⁻¹
1668 CULPEPPER & COLE *Barthol. Anat.* I. xiii. 30 It goes by little and little straight forward, and is silently terminated towards the spleen.

How many definitions of "silently" are there in the dictionary entry above?

- Ⓐ 3
- Ⓑ 4
- Ⓒ 1
- Ⓓ 2

Question Number: 4

Veteran.— N. veteran, old man, seer, patriarch, graybeard; grandfather, grandsire; grandam; gaffer, gammer; crone; pantaloon; sexagenarian, octogenarian, nonagenarian, centenarian; old stager; dotard &c. 501. preadamite[obs3], Methuselah, Nestor, old Parr; elders; forefathers &c. (paternity) 166. Phr. "superfluous lags the veteran on the stage" [Johnson].

According to the thesaurus entry above, what is a synonym for the word, "veteran?"

Ⓐ **veterinarian**
Ⓑ **graybeard**
Ⓒ **young man**
Ⓓ **None of the above**

Question Number: 5

Skeletal (ske·lᵻ́tăl), a. [f. SKELET-ON sb. + -AL.] Of or belonging to, forming or formed by, forming part of, or resembling, a skeleton.
Skeletal muscle, a muscle attached to and controlling a part of a skeleton.
1854 OWEN in *Orr's Circ. Sci., Org. Nat.* I. 168 The skeletal framework..does not go beyond the fibrous stage. 1872 HUMPHRY *Myology* 8 The skeletal formations in the sternal region of the visceral wall. 1877 M. FOSTER *Physiol.* I. ii. (1879) 37 All the ordinary striated skeletal muscles are connected with nerves.

What is the definition of "skeletal?"

Ⓐ **A bodily system made of muscle and bones, the most important systems in the body.**
Ⓑ **Made of bones**
Ⓒ **The skeletal region of the visceral wall**
Ⓓ **Of or belonging to, forming or formed by, forming part of, or resembling, a skeleton**

Question Number: 6

Edge. — N. edge, verge, brink, brow, brim, margin, border, confine, skirt, rim, flange, side, mouth; jaws, chops, chaps, fauces; lip, muzzle. threshold, door, porch; portal &c. (opening) 260; coast, shore. frame, fringe, flounce, frill, list, trimming, edging, skirting, hem, selvedge, welt, furbelow, valance, gimp. Adj. border, marginal, skirting; labial, labiated[obs3], marginated[obs3].

Which of the following is NOT a synonym for "edge?"

Ⓐ **brink**
Ⓑ **flank**
Ⓒ **verge**
Ⓓ **rim**

Question Number: 7

Sitar (si·tāɹ). *Anglo-Ind.* Also **sitarre**. [Urdū
سِتار *sitār.*] A form of guitar, properly having
three strings, used in India.
1845 STOCQUELER *Hdbk. Brit. India* (1854) 26 A trio of
sitars, or rude violins. **1859** J. LANG *Wand. India* 152 Two
or three of the company..played alternately on the sitarre
(native guitar or violin). **1879** E. ARNOLD *Lt. Asia* VI. 144
One that twitched A three-string sitar. **1898** SIR G. ROBERT-
SON *Chitral* i. 7 A sitar-player will sing of love.
Si·tarch. *rare⁻⁰.* [ad. Gr. σιτάρχης or σιτ-
αρχος, f. σῖτος corn, food.] (See quots.)
1656 BLOUNT *Glossgr., Sitarch,* he that hath the Office to
provide Corn, and Victuals sufficient. **1676** COLES, *Sitarch,*
a Pourveyor.

Where might one see a sitar?

Ⓐ **A hospital**
Ⓑ **A construction site**
Ⓒ **An international music festival**
Ⓓ **All of the above**

Question Number: 8

Sky·scape. [f. SKY *sb.*¹, after *landscape,
seascape.*] A view of the sky; also in painting,
etc., a representation of part of the sky.
1817 SOUTHEY *Let.* in *Life* (1850) IV. 283 It was the un-
broken horizon which impressed me,... and the skyscapes
which it afforded. **1861** C. J. ANDERSON *Okavango* x. 137
The beautiful and striking skyscapes and atmospheric
coruscations attendant on these storms. **1878** GROSART
More's Poems Introd. p. xli, The great ancient Painters,
whose backgrounds of portraits..rather than land-scape,
or sea-scape, or sky-scape proper, assure us [etc.].

Which of the following is not a meaning of the word, "skyscape?"

Ⓐ **Escaping by way of the sky**
Ⓑ **A view of the sky**
Ⓒ **A representation of part of the sky in painting, etc.**
Ⓓ **B & C**

Question Number: 9

Notch. — N. notch, dent, nick, cut; indent, indentation; dimple. embrasure, battlement, machicolation[obs3]; saw, tooth, crenelle[obs3], scallop, scollop[obs3], vandyke; depression; jag. V. notch, nick, cut, dent, indent, jag, scarify, scotch, crimp, scallop, scollop[obs3], crenulate[obs3], vandyke. Adj. notched &c. v.; crenate[obs3], crenated[obs3]; dentate, dentated; denticulate, denticulated; toothed, palmated[obs3], serrated.

Which of the following synonyms for "notch" is a verb?

Ⓐ **nick**
Ⓑ **embrasure**
Ⓒ **toothed**
Ⓓ **None of the Above**

Question Number: 10

Slog (slog), *v.* *colloq.* [Of obscure origin. Cf. SLUG *v.*[4]]

1. *trans.* To hit or strike hard; to drive with blows. Also *fig.*, to assail violently.

1853 'C. BEDE' *Verdant Green* xi. 106 His whole person [had been] put in chancery, stung, bruised, fibbed,…slogged, and otherwise ill-treated. 1884 'R. BOLDREWOOD' *Melb. Memories* iv. 32 We slogged the tired cattle round the fence. 1891 *Spectator* 10 Oct. 487/1 They love snubbing their friends and 'slogging' their enemies.

b. *Cricket.* To obtain (runs) by hard hitting.

1897 H. W. BLEAKLEY *Short Innings* iii. 49 Mr. Dolly slogged sixes and fours until he had made about eighty.

2. *intr.* To walk heavily or doggedly.

Halliwell's '*Slog*, to lag behind' probably belongs to SLUG *v.* 1872 CALVERLEY *Fly Leaves* (1903) 119 Then *shiit*…off slogs boy. 1876 *Mid-Yorksh. Gloss.*, *Slog*, to walk with burdened feet, as through snow, or puddle. 1907 *Westm. Gaz.* 2 Oct. 2/1 Overtaking the guns, we 'slogged' on with them for a mile or more.

3. To deal heavy blows, to work hard (*at* something), to labour *away*, etc.

1888 *Daily News* 22 May 5/2, I slogged at it, day in and day out. 1894 HESLOP *Northumberland Gloss.* s.v., They slogged away at the anchor shank. 1903 *19th Cent.* Mar. 392 They have no incentives to slog and slave.

Which of the following is NOT a definition of the word, "slog?"

Ⓐ To hit or strike hard
Ⓑ To walk heavily or doggedly
Ⓒ To deal heavy blows, to work hard
Ⓓ None of the above

Similes and Metaphors (L.4.5.A)

Question Number: 1

The sky was an angry, purple monster. It roared fiercely as the thunder crashed and rain poured down.

What does the metaphor in the first sentence mean?

Ⓐ **The sky had clouds in the shape of a monster.**
Ⓑ **The sky was stormy.**
Ⓒ **Monsters invaded the town.**
Ⓓ **None of the above**

Question Number: 2

In the days after Dad was laid off almost everyone was gloomy. Sam didn't smile, <u>Mom hovered over everyone like a cloud full of rain</u>. It was Sasha who was the ray of sunshine when she declared, "It's alright. Hugs are free!"

What purpose does the author's simile serve in the paragraph?

Ⓐ **It describes the setting after Dad was laid off.**
Ⓑ **It makes the point that mom was gloomy and likely to cry.**
Ⓒ **It shows that Sasha was a happy, upbeat presence in the house.**
Ⓓ **It reminds us that hugs are free.**

Question Number: 3

The starting goalie was out with an injury, so Kevin was finally getting his chance to prove his worth. He knew he could do it. He was ready. Kevin was a brick wall.

By comparing Kevin to a brick wall, what is the speaker trying to say about Kevin?

Ⓐ **He would not allow anyone to score on him.**
Ⓑ **He was hard-headed.**
Ⓒ **He built a wall in front of his soccer goal.**
Ⓓ **He threw bricks at his opponent.**

Question Number: 4

In the days after Dad was laid off almost everyone was gloomy. Sam didn't smile, Mom hovered over everyone like a cloud full of rain. <u>It was Sasha who was the ray of sunshine when she declared, "It's alright. Hugs are free!"</u>

What purpose does the author's metaphor serve in the paragraph?

Ⓐ **It describes the setting after Dad was laid off.**
Ⓑ **It makes the point that mom was a gloomy and likely to cry.**
Ⓒ **It shows that Sasha was a happy, upbeat presence in the house.**
Ⓓ **It reminds us that hugs are free.**

Question Number: 5

<u>Their family was like a patchwork quilt</u> of nationalities and colors. Each adopted child added something beautiful to the whole.

What does the simile in the above paragraph mean?

Ⓐ Like a patchwork quilt, the family was old and ragged. It was probably time to throw it out.

Ⓑ Their family had old-fashioned traditions, like a patchwork quilt from generations past.

Ⓒ Like a patchwork quilt, the children were adopted by parents who loved them very much.

Ⓓ Like a patchwork quilt that has bits of different fabric stitched together, the family had children of different nationalities and colors bound together as brothers and sisters. The overall effect was beautiful.

Question Number: 6

The ballerinas were like swans gliding over the stage.
Why does the speaker compare ballerinas to swans?

Ⓐ To show that they were white
Ⓑ To show that they squawked like birds
Ⓒ To show that they can swim
Ⓓ To show that they are graceful and elegant

Question Number: 7

Which similes below would be helpful in describing a terrified look on someone's face?

Ⓐ Her eyes drooped like wilted flowers, and her hands hung limp like wet spaghetti noodles.

Ⓑ Her eyes were as sharp as arrows, and her fists clenched tight like hammers waiting to strike.

Ⓒ Her eyes were soft like a morning dew, and her hands lay still as resting cherubs.

Ⓓ Her eyes were as big as sewer lids, and her hands trembled like tiny earthquakes.

Question Number: 8

Which metaphor below would be helpful in describing a presentation that went terribly?

(A) In that moment Alfonso was a lion tamer, and the crowd was a well-trained pride eating from the palm of his hand.

(B) In that moment Alfonso was the conductor of a train that was steady on its rails and going full steam ahead.

(C) In that moment Alfonso was a bright flame, and the people gathered like moths around him.

(D) In that moment Alfonso was the captain of an ill-fated voyage, and he was going down with his ship.

Question Number: 9

Which simile below would help describe a child's joy in being reunited with a mother returning from a military tour of duty in another country?

(A) Hannah's face lit up like fireworks on the Fourth of July when she glimpsed her mother rounding the corner. It was really her!

(B) Hannah closed up like a locked bedroom door when she saw her mother for the first time.

(C) Hannah pounded her fist on the counter like it was a judge's ruinous gavel when she saw her mother rounding the corner.

(D) Hannah's eyes turned down, and her face turned red as a beet when she glimpsed her mother for the first time.

Question Number: 10

Which metaphor below would be helpful in describing a huge crowd of people at a festival?

(A) The people marched through the streets with purpose, like an army marching toward battle.

(B) The streets were a barren desert, and the music echoed off of empty storefronts.

(C) A sea of delighted people swept over the sidewalks and into the street as they passed from attraction to attraction.

(D) I was on an emotional roller coaster on the day of the festival.

Idiomatic Expressions and Proverbs (L.4.5.B)

Question Number: 1

If Wendy's dad found out she took her cell phone to school, he would _hit the ceiling_.

What is meant by the idiom _hit the ceiling_ in the above sentence?

Ⓐ Wendy's dad will jump high.
Ⓑ Wendy's dad will be very angry.
Ⓒ Wendy's dad will laugh loudly.
Ⓓ Wendy's dad will congratulate her.

Question Number: 2

I think you need to swallow your pride and apologize to your teacher for talking in class.

What is meant by the idiom swallow your pride?

Ⓐ To swallow hard
Ⓑ To deny doing something
Ⓒ To forget about being embarrassed
Ⓓ To pretend you are sorry

Question Number: 3

Mindy was walking on air after she went backstage and met Adam Levine.

What does the idiom 'walking on air' mean?

Ⓐ Mindy was floating through the air.
Ⓑ Mindy was dreaming.
Ⓒ Mindy was in a state of bliss.
Ⓓ Mindy was disappointed.

Question Number: 4

I am not sure how long I will stay at the dance. I'm going to play it by ear.

What is the meaning of '_play it by ear_' in the above sentence?

Ⓐ Play a musical instrument without sheet music
Ⓑ Decide as you see how things go rather than making plans
Ⓒ Listen for someone to tell you what to do
Ⓓ Think carefully before making a decision

Question Number: 5

After winning a million dollars, Kelly was running around like a chicken with its head cut off.

What does the idiom 'like a chicken with its head cut off' mean?

Ⓐ **To act in a calm manner**
Ⓑ **To be bleeding profusely**
Ⓒ **To run around clucking and flapping your arms**
Ⓓ **To act in a frenzied manner**

Question Number: 6

Jackie was not very happy. Not only did she lose her favorite necklace, but she also learned that her best friend was going to sleep-away camp for the whole summer while she had to go to summer school. Jackie really felt down in the dumps.

What does "down in the dumps mean" in the sentence?

Ⓐ **sad**
Ⓑ **bringing the garbage to the end of the driveway**
Ⓒ **excited**
Ⓓ **flabbergasted**

Question Number: 7

Amy's aunt spent months knitting a scarf for Amy. When Amy received the present and looked at it, she really didn't like the colors. She couldn't let her aunt know she was disappointed after all her hard work, so she told a little white lie instead.

What does a "little white lie" mean in the sentence?

Ⓐ **huge made up story**
Ⓑ **truth**
Ⓒ **lie that is told to avoid hurting someone's feelings**
Ⓓ **the lie was painted white**

Question Number: 8

The renovations the Johnsons were making on the house were getting too expensive. The Johnsons wanted the best of the best, but they didn't have enough money to pay for it all. Their architect came to speak with them. "You have some great ideas, but we're going to need to see where we can cut corners. We may have to change some of the original plans to save some money; otherwise we won't be able to finish the house."

What does "cut corners" mean in the sentence?

Ⓐ cut the edges of the play's program
Ⓑ clip some coupons
Ⓒ use money wisely and try to save by spending only what is necessary
Ⓓ mow the lawn

Question Number: 9

What does the idiom "Half a loaf is better than none" mean?

Ⓐ You can't judge a person's character by how he or she looks.
Ⓑ You usually do better than others if you get there ahead of others.
Ⓒ This means having something is better than not having anything at all.
Ⓓ Mind your own business and let others mind theirs.

Question Number: 10

What does the idiom "Beauty is only skin deep" mean?

Ⓐ If something unfortunate happens, it usually won't happen again.
Ⓑ Take care of a small problem before it becomes a big one.
Ⓒ A picture can explain things better than words.
Ⓓ You can't judge a person's character by how he or she looks.

Question Number: 1

Choose the correct set of synonyms for "_small_."

Ⓐ enormous, giant
Ⓑ minute, gargantuan
Ⓒ small, unseen
Ⓓ miniature, minute

Question Number: 2

Choose the correct set of _synonyms_.

Ⓐ unrealistic, believable
Ⓑ noteworthy, important
Ⓒ noteworthy, insignificant
Ⓓ unfair, just

Question Number: 3

Choose the correct set of _antonyms_.

Ⓐ radiant, dull
Ⓑ rescue, save
Ⓒ chortle, laugh
Ⓓ sparkle, shine

Question Number: 4

Choose the synonym for "_happy_."

Ⓐ miserable
Ⓑ ecstatic
Ⓒ subdued
Ⓓ wretched

Question Number: 5

Choose the correct set of antonyms for "_pretty_."

Ⓐ repulsive, unattractive
Ⓑ lovely, handsome
Ⓒ enticing, glamour
Ⓓ appealing, grotesque

Question Number: 6

What is a synonym for the word, "chaos?"

Ⓐ huge
Ⓑ agree
Ⓒ disorder
Ⓓ famous

Question Number: 7

Find the correct set of synonyms below.

Ⓐ fat and aged
Ⓑ tend and thick
Ⓒ fat and thick
Ⓓ aged and tend

Question Number: 8

Find the correct set of antonyms below.

Ⓐ peculiar and general
Ⓑ peculiar and common
Ⓒ general and included
Ⓓ general and common

Question Number: 9

What would be a good antonym for the word, "recall?"

Ⓐ contend
Ⓑ assert
Ⓒ forget
Ⓓ urge

Question Number: 10

What is an antonym for the word, "active?"

Ⓐ lazy
Ⓑ energetic
Ⓒ healthy
Ⓓ running

Academic and Domain Specific 4th Grade Words (L.4.6)

Question Number: 1

When Jeremy arrived home his mom _____ him about the dance until he could think of no more details to give her.

Choose the word that best completes the sentence.

Ⓐ Yelled at
Ⓑ quizzed
Ⓒ praised
Ⓓ waddled

Question Number: 2

The woodlands of the midatlantic region are filled with all sorts of interesting _____.
Choose the word that best completes the sentence.

Ⓐ movies
Ⓑ wildlife
Ⓒ colleges
Ⓓ mortar

Question Number: 3

_____ John Muir helped preserve our country's natural beauty by helping to establish Yosemite National Park.

Choose the word that best completes sentence.

Ⓐ Antagoinist
Ⓑ Pianist
Ⓒ Conservationist
Ⓓ Statistician

Question Number: 4

Sarah was _____ at the news that the giant oak she had worked to protect was going to be removed in order to build a parking lot.

Choose the word that best completes the sentence.

Ⓐ crestfallen
Ⓑ starstruck
Ⓒ jovial
Ⓓ greedy

Question Number: 5

When an animal is _____ the government will sometimes place restrictions on hunting it.

Choose the word that best completes the sentence.

Ⓐ rabid
Ⓑ thretening
Ⓒ special
Ⓓ endangered

Question Number: 6

"Mommmmm, do I haaaaaave to?" Lester _____ as his mother sat across the table with her eyes trained on his Brussels sprouts.

Choose the word that best completes the sentence.

Ⓐ said
Ⓑ called
Ⓒ shrieked
Ⓓ whined

Question Number: 7

"Wha-wha-what was th-that?" Dera _____ as she climbed the creaky stairs in the old house.

Choose the word that best completes the sentence.

Ⓐ commanded
Ⓑ announced
Ⓒ stammered
Ⓓ laughed

Question Number: 8

My _____ is that the celery's stalk turned blue because it absorbed the colored water in the vase.

Ⓐ idea
Ⓑ intuition
Ⓒ guess
Ⓓ hypothesis

Question Number: 9

Monica _____ Peter's reasoning by referring to an example in the text that did not support the idea he suggested.

Ⓐ agreed
Ⓑ dissed
Ⓒ critiqued
Ⓓ slammed

Question Number: 10

When putting forth an idea about what a character is thinking, it is best to use _____ from the text.

Choose the word that best completes the sentence.

Ⓐ characters
Ⓑ evidence
Ⓒ chapters
Ⓓ nonfiction

End of Language

Answer Key and Detailed Explanations

Language

Pronouns (L.4.1.A)

Question No.	Answer	Detailed Explanation
1	B	'We' refers to Bobby and the author. While 'us' could also refer to both Bobby and the author, it is not the correct pronoun for this set of sentences.
2	A	'He' is the correct pronoun for this sentence set. One way to check this is to take out the words 'and his father' from the sentence and see if it still makes sense.
3	A	'He' refers to Jamie which makes it the correct pronoun in this sentence.
4	C	'Their' is a possessive pronoun. It refers to the dogs' possession.
5	D	'Her' is a possessive pronoun. It refers to the girl's possession so it is the correct pronoun to use.
6	C	'Their' is a possessive pronoun and 'their' refers to the dancers.
7	A	'Her' is a possessive pronoun. Because the sentence set refers to the sister's first dance, a possessive pronoun is the correct choice.
8	C	'They' is the subject of the sentence. Since the sentence has the word together, we know more than one person is involved.
9	D	'Her' is the correct choice. Although him' would also work in the sentence correctly, the second sentence refers to the teacher as a female, so 'her' is most correct.
10	B	'They' refers correctly to Alice and Jennifer. Although A and C also refer to more than one person, 'they' is most accurate.

Progressive Verb Tense (L.4.1.B)

1	B	Efrain is the subject of the sentence. Since he will be traveling to Europe in the future, the future progressive tense is correct.
2	D	Darrel and I are the subjects of the sentence. Since there is a plural subject, 'will attend' is the correct verb.
3	A	Since Minnie, Jill, and Sandra are singing presently, use the present progressive tense.

Question No.	Answer	Detailed Explanation
4	C	The girls are failing to plan in the present, so present progressive tense is correct.
5	B	Jenny is working now to earn money; so she is saving in the present progressive tense.
6	B	The cheerleading was ongoing in the past; so use the past progressive tense.
7	C	The trees are presently engaged in the ongoing action of waving in the wind. Our evidence for this is the verb *show* later in the sentence. Therefore, the present progressive must be used.
8	C	Change in the sentence is ongoing and is happening now, so we use the present progressive tense.
9	B	She was engaged in the ongoing act of sitting when the waiter approached, so we use the past progressive tense.
10	C	Kenji and Briana's parents will pick them up in the future, so future progressive tense is appropriate.

Modal Auxiliary Verbs (L.4.1.C)

1	D	"Will" in sentence 3 and "may" in sentence 4 are both modal auxiliary verbs. These modal auxiliaries are connected to ideas of doubt or probability of future events.
2	B	Modal auxiliaries can be used for each of these purposes; but in this case it is uncertain whether or not Oliver's fever will go away.
3	D	"Could" is the correct answer choice. It is being used to express a past possibility.
4	C	"Had" is the modal auxiliary verb. It is being used to affirm that Dana had no choice about leaving the party.
5	A	"Shouldn't" is the modal auxiliary verb. It is being used to give advice.
6	D	"Could" is the modal auxiliary verb. It is being used in this sentence to express possibility.
7	C	"Shall" is a form of "will" and is the modal auxiliary verb. It is being used to express a decision or promise the speaker has made.
8	D	"Would" is a better choice, because it is not certain that the speaker will ever interview Maya Angelou.
9	B	By asking if she "can" hand him the apple, Marvin is really asking if she is capable. He should use the auxiliary modal verb "will" instead if he wants her to actually do the action.

Question No.	Answer	Detailed Explanation
10	A	"Might" is used correctly in the first choice to express uncertainty about a future event. Choice B lacks a verb after "shall." Choice C should read, "She must remember…"

Adjectives and Adverbs (L.4.1.D)

1	C	Frequently is the adverb modifying 'visits'. It answers the question when.
2	B	Beautiful modifies park. It answers the question what kind.
3	D	Cold is an adjective in the sentence. It is modifying 'it'.
4	B	Choice B is the correct option. This choice uses the most appropriate order of adverbs and adjectives according to conventional patterns.
5	B	*Fastest* is the superlative adjective that completes the sentence.
6	D	Excited is the adjective that modifies Lindsay, Laine, and John. In the question stem: "Each put their things" mixes singular & plural. Should be "They put their things…" or "Each put his or her things…"
7	C	Most beautiful is the correct superlative adjective that modifies girl.
8	D	Colder is a comparative adjective.
9	D	Most horrific is the correct superlative adjective that completes the sentence.
10	B	Hungrily and stealthily are the adverbs that modify the verb walked and are in the correct order.

Prepositional Phrases (L.4.1.E)

1	B	"Into the pool" and "of cool water" are both prepositional phrases.
2	D	"Underneath" is the preposition. Journals is the object of the preposition.
3	C	"For school" and "without your lunchbox" are both prepositional phrases.
4	A	"On the rug" is the prepositional phrase.
5	D	"At the fair" is the prepositional phrase.
6	C	"Into the room" and "in his favorite chair" are both prepositional phrases.

Question No.	Answer	Detailed Explanation
7	D	"Across" is the preposition, and "yard" is the object of the preposition.
8	B	"From the kitchen" is the prepositional phrase.
9	A	There are not prepositional phrases in the first choice.
10	C	"Down" is the preposition, and "trail" is the object of the preposition.

Complete Sentences (L.4.1.F)

1	A	The first answer choice makes the run-on sentence into a compound sentence by adding a comma and the coordinating conjunction, "but." This is appropriate because both parts of the sentence have a subject and predicate.
2	B	The second choice is correct. This resolves the run-on sentence by creating a compound sentence followed by a second complete sentence with a subject and predicate.
3	C	The third answer choice is correct. All other sentences have subjects and predicates, but the third choice is a dependent clause.
4	C	The third answer choice is correct. As is, the sentence has no verb. The subject is "ways." Adding "There are," gives this sentence a verb and makes it complete.
5	C	The third answer choice is correct. This sentence lacks a subject, most likely "Synthesis."
6	D	The fourth answer choice is correct. The editor noticed that the 2nd "sentence" in the paragraph was actually a dependent clause, not a complete sentence. He solved the problem by combining it with the first sentence.
7	A	The first answer choice is correct. This choice contains two complete sentences that are not joined by a comma and coordinating conjunction.
8	D	The fourth answer choice is correct. It is tempting to say the second sentence is a run-on, but it is one complete sentence with a compound predicate.
9	B	The second choice is correct. "A really great pair of shoes," is the complete subject and, "should be both stylish and comfortable," is the complete predicate.
10	A	The first answer choice is correct. It consists of a dependent clause and an independent clause separated by a comma. Choices B and C are fragments, and Choice D is a run-on sentence.

Frequently Confused Words (L.4.1.G)

Question No.	Answer	Detailed Explanation
1	A	The first answer choice is correct. "Their" shows owner-ship.
2	C	The third choice is correct. "There" refers to a place.
3	B	The second answer choice is correct. The contraction, "they're" means "they are."
4	C	The third choice is correct. "To" should replace "too" because it is being used as a preposition before "my grandmother's house." "Too" is incorrect because it means "also," which would not make sense in this sentence.
5	C	The third answer choice is correct. "Were" is a verb that does not make sense in the sentence, but "where" references place.
6	B	The second choice is correct. The contraction, "we're," means "we are."
7	A	The first answer choice is correct. "Breathe" is a verb, but "breath" is a noun.
8	D	The fourth answer choice is correct. "Passed" is the verb meaning he successfully took his test. "Past" refers to time.
9	B	The second choice is correct. "Accept" means "to take," while "except" means "to leave out."
10	B	The second choice is correct. In this case the principal is the most important person in the school. A principle is a commonly held truth.

How is it Capitalized? (L.4.2.A)

1	B	Holidays and months should be capitalized. The names of seasons should not.
2	A	Titles, initials, and names of people should all be capitalized.
3	D	Street names should be capitalized.
4	A	Names of cities and abbreviations for states should be capitalized.
5	B	"Semester" is not a proper noun and should not be capitalized. Names of school classes that are proper adjectives (related to a proper noun such as a country) should be capitalized.

Question No.	Answer	Detailed Explanation
6	B	The first word of a title and all important words in a title should be capitalized.
7	C	Titles, people's names, family terms when followed by a person's name, and family terms used as a person's name are all capitalized.
8	C	The first word of a closing of a letter should be capitalized. A person's first and last name should be capitalized.
9	D	The first word of a sentence should be capitalized. Names of rivers and landmarks should be capitalized.
10	C	Brand names of products should be capitalized.

What's the Punctuation? (L.4.2.B/C)

1	D	The fourth choice is the only sentence that is punctuated correctly.
2	D	Use commas and quotation marks to mark direct speech.
3	B	Commas are used before the coordinating conjunction in a compound sentence. The comma in the sentence is not needed. It is not a compound sentence because it has only one subject.
4	A	Use commas on other punctuations to match direct speech.
5	B	Use quotation marks and a comma to mark direct speech.
6	A	There are no errors in the sentence. The writer is merely explaining what the teacher asked, not quoting him directly.
7	A	The first choice is correct because it uses commas to introduce a quotation from a text.
8	C	The third choice is correct because it uses commas to introduce a quotation from a text.
9	D	The fourth choice is correct because it uses commas to introduce a quotation from a text.
10	D	The fourth choice uses a comma before the coordinating conjunction in a compound sentence.

How is it Spelled? (L.4.2.D)

Question No.	Answer	Detailed Explanation
1	D	*Clarify* is the correctly spelled word that best fits the sentence. *Carefully* is also spelled correctly, but it does not make sense in the sentence.
2	B	*Vehicle* is the correct spelling.
3	A	*Pollution* is the correct spelling.
4	C	*Believe* is the correct spelling.
5	D	*Monkeys, strawberries,* and *cherries* are the correct spellings of the other choices.
6	B	*Knives* is the correct spelling for the plural form of knife.
7	A	*Collateral* is the correct spelling.
8	D	*Separately* is the correct spelling.
9	B	*Boxes* is the correct spelling.
10	D	*Narrate* is the correctly spelled word.

Word Choice: Attending to Precision (L.4.3.A)

1	B	"Strutted" makes the most sense in the sentence. Although all choices are verbs that could describe how a person enters a room, "strutted" conveys a sense of pride.
2	B	"Grueling" means extremely tiring and demanding. While the job may be described as "uncomfortable," "grueling" describes the work more precisely, based the context in the second sentence.
3	C	"Elated" is the most precise word choice. The second sentence gives context indicating that Dante was excited about his award.
4	A	"Gigantic" makes the most sense in this sentence. While "big" could also describe the mess, it is not as precise. "Gigantic" gives the reader an idea of how big the mess was.
5	B	"Damaging" is the best answer choice because it indicates that this evidence hurt the defendant's case, leading to her conviction.
6	D	"Fireball" makes the most sense in the sentence. A "ham" is someone who likes to entertain people by being funny; a "scrooge" is miserly, and a "shrinking violet" is bashful. A "fireball" is feisty.

Question No.	Answer	Detailed Explanation
7	D	"Clambered" is the most precise word for the sentence. To clamber means to climb, move, or get in or out of something in an awkward or laborious way. This is how a frenzied girl might move through a crowd of people to see a boy band.
8	D	The fourth answer choice is most precise. Waterfalls are more likely to be described as "cascading" than any of the other less precise answer choices.
9	C	"Reduces" is a more precise word to help explain that recycling eliminates some landfill waste.
10	A	Squealing is a noise a very excited person might make, and Janet was excited by the news she was sharing.

Punctuating for Effect! (L.4.3.B)

1	D	The fourth answer choice is correct. In the first choice there are no quotation marks to mark speech; the second choice implies a third person is speaking; and the third choice would need an apostrophe "s" after "Jermaine" (with a lower case "m") in order to be correct.
2	B	The second answer choice is correct. It is the only choice that implies another character is speaking, and it has an exclamation point at the end to indicate excitement or shouting.
3	C	An exclamation point is the correct way to end this sentence. Dante is very excited about his award.
4	D	The fourth answer choice is correct. This is neither a question, nor an exclamatory sentence. The third answer choice has no end punctuation.
5	A	The first answer choice is correct. A period is appropriate end punctuation for a declarative sentence or statement.
6	B	The second choice is correct. An exclamation point is appropriate when punctuating an interjection, which "Sheesh!" is in the second sentence.
7	C	The third choice is correct. The third sentence asks a question.
8	B	The second choice is correct. An exclamation point is appropriate end punctuation for the interjection, "Wow!" which expresses surprise and excitement.

Question No.	Answer	Detailed Explanation
9	C	The third choice is correct. It is incorrect to end a question with an exclamation point. The other answer choices use the exclamation point to imply excitement or add emphasis on the sentence.
10	A	The first choice is correct. The exclamation point implies excitement in the sentence.

Finding the Meaning (L.4.3.C)

1	B	Extracted means took out. The milk is taken out of the co-conut.
2	C	After losing everything in a fire, a person would be really sad and upset. Despairing means very sad.
3	B	We know that it means comfort, because dad did it after the girl's dog died.
4	D	We know the kittens are in bed against their mother, so it means "snuggled up to."
5	B	"In wide-eyed astonishment" is the clue that lets us know it means astonished, and "stared stupidly" most closly matches the "gawked at".
6	D	Cease means stop.
7	B	We know that weary means tired, because the man biked for a very long time.
8	D	We know they rested on the bleachers, so lounged means relaxed.
9	D	We know he went from the top of the bleachers to the ground, so plummeted means plunged.
10	B	Since the writer is packing cold weather clothes, we know that frigid means freezing.

Context Clues (L.4.4.A)

1	B	"Sentiment," is a view or attitude toward a situation or event, in this case the suffering of Americans during the Great Depression. Roosevelt's view was that the biggest obstacle to progress was fear. The other answer choices do not make sense in the paragraph.
2	B	"Assuage," means "to ease." The words Roosevelt shared in his speech helped ease people's fear. The second sentence says, "giving them hope." This provides context that assuage is a positive word and that Roosevelt made them feel better, not worse.

Question No.	Answer	Detailed Explanation
3	B	"Affluent" means wealthy or having a lot of money. Context clues are that the food was expensive and patrons had to dress nicely.
4	D	"Patrons" are customers. The context clue is that they had to, "dress nicely in <u>order to eat there</u>." The customers of a restaurant are the people who eat there, unlike the cooks or the waiters. "Doctors" is unrelated to the clues in the paragraph.
5	B	A "miser" is someone who wishes to spend as little money as possible. The definition is included in the sentence.
6	D	"Devoid" means lacking or without. The clue is that, "he does not have any true friends to speak of."
7	D	A "corridor" is a hallway. Context clues describe the corridor as "long" and as having "door after door." Long hallways in hospitals are lined with doors.
8	D	In this paragraph, "earnest" refers to Hazel's state of mind. She was serious about making patients smile.
9	D	"Invest" means to give someone money with the intention of making money. Marcus was expecting Mel and Deena to repay him the ten dollars plus ten percent of each cup they sold.
10	A	"Reimburse" means to repay. Marcus expected Mel and Deena to repay him the money he lent them to use to buy supplies for their lemonade stand. The clue in the text is "plus ten percent of each cup they sell."

The Meaning of Words (L.4.4.B)

1	B	"Dis-" is a prefix meaning *not or opposite of*.
2	C	"Re-" is a prefix that means *again*.
3	B	"Hemi" is a prefix that means *half*, so *hemisphere* refers to half of the earth.
4	C	The prefix "sub" means *below*
5	B	The prefix "hyper" means *excessive*.
6	C	Adding the suffix -ology (which means "study of")to the root word geo creates the new word geology, which means study of the earth
7	D	All of the other choices use an affix to change the meaning of the word.
8	D	"Able" is a Latin suffix meaning capable or worthy of.

Question No.	Answer	Detailed Explanation
9	C	Tract is the root word, because it can stand alone. The Latin meaning is to pull, drag, or draw.
10	A	While each of the words in the list contain Greek roots, only option A's root word means time. 'Chron' means time. It can also be found in the word chronological, like putting events in chronological order in a timeline for example.

For Your Reference (L.4.4.C)

1	A	The first choice is correct. Textbook glossaries contain definitions of key words in the textbook.
2	D	The fourth choice is correct. The "N" at the beginning of the entry tells the reader this.
3	D	There are 2 definitions in the entry for "silently." They are numbered in bold, with the most common definition listed first.
4	B	The second choice is correct. The entry word in a thesaurus is followed by the part of speech and a list of synonyms. Antonyms are also frequently listed after that.
5	D	The fourth choice is correct. The definition appears after the pronunciation.
6	B	The second choice is correct. It is the only word not listed as a synonym.
7	C	The third choice is correct. Because the sitar is a) an instrument, and b) used in India, an international music festival is the most likely place to see one.
8	A	The first choice is correct. It is the only definition not found in the entry above.
9	A	"Nick" is the only synonym above listed after the "V." "Embasure" is a noun, while "toothed" is an adjective.
10	D	The answer choice D is correct. Each of the three definitions in the answer choices are accurate, "None of the above" would NOT be a definition of slog because all choices are real.

Similes and Metaphors (L.4.5.A)

Question No.	Answer	Detailed Explanation
1	B	The second answer choice is correct. The metaphor compares the sky to an angry monster. They are both purple, the thunder sounds like roaring. Like a monster, the stormy sky is fierce and threatening.
2	B	The simile describes Mom as being like a rain cloud. Rain clouds are dark and gloomy, which matches Mom's mood.
3	A	Brick walls are strong and do not allow objects to pass through them. By comparing Kevin to a brick wall, he is saying Kevin will not allow his opponent to score.
4	C	The metaphor compares Sasha to a ray of sunshine. Sunshine is considered happy like Sasha was when she looked on the bright side of the situation.
5	D	The fourth answer choice is correct. It best explains the meaning of the simile. The other answer choices are not supported by the context in the paragraph.
6	D	Ballerinas are dancers, and swans are birds. The speaker uses the simile to compare their movement, which is graceful and elegant. The word, "gliding," supports this comparison.
7	D	The fourth answer choice is correct. When someone is terrified, their eyes often widen and their hands might tremble. The first answer choice seems to describe someone sad or hopeless, the second is determined and powerful, and the third is peaceful or kind.
8	D	The fourth answer choice is correct. This is the only metaphor that does not describe Alfonso as in-control, steady, or charismatic. Instead it likens him to the captain of a sinking ship.
9	A	The first answer choice is correct. It is the only choice that paints a joyous picture of the reunion between a daughter and her mother.
10	C	The third answer choice is correct. It is the only choice that is a) a metaphor, b) describes the crowd, and c) describes the way a crowd would behave at a festival—a jovial, happy occasion.

Idiomatic Expressions and Proverbs (L.4.5.B)

Question No.	Answer	Detailed Explanation
1	B	"Hit the ceiling" means get very angry.
2	C	"Swallow your pride" means to ignore your pride and do something anyway.
3	C	"Walking on air" means really happy.
4	B	"Play it by ear" means figure out things as you go.
5	D	"Like a chicken with its head cut off" means running around wildly.
6	A	"Down in the dumps" means really sad and depressed.
7	C	"A little white lie" means a lie that is not meant to hurt anyone.
8	C	"Cut corners" means to take shortcuts.
9	C	"Half a loaf is better than none" means to appreciate what you have instead of wanting more.
10	D	"Beauty is only skin deep" means that true beauty is based on personality.

Synonyms and Antonyms (L.4.5.C)

1	D	"Miniature" and "minute" are synonyms of "small." Synonyms are words that mean the same thing.
2	B	"Noteworthy" and "important" are synonyms, or words that mean the same.
3	A	"Radiant" and "dull" are antonyms, or words that mean the opposite.
4	B	"Ecstatic" and "happy" are synonyms, or words that mean the same.
5	A	"Repulsive" and "unattractive" are antonyms for "pretty." Antonyms are words that mean the opposite.
6	C	"Chaos" and "disorder" are synonyms, or words that mean the same.
7	C	"Fat" and "thick" are synonyms, or words that mean the same.
8	B	"Peculiar" and "common" are antonyms, or words that mean the opposite.
9	C	"Recall" and "forget" are antonyms, or words that mean the opposite.

Question No.	Answer	Detailed Explanation
10	A	"Active" and "lazy" are antonyms, or words that mean the opposite.

Academic and Domain Specific 4th Grade Words (L.4.6)

1	B	"Quizzed" makes the most sense in the sentence. It means she questioned him for details about the dance.
2	B	"Wildlife," meaning plants and animals, is the best choice. None of the other answer choices make sense.
3	C	"Conservationist," meaning someone who works to preserve wildlife, is the best choice here. The other choices make no sense in the sentence.
4	A	"Crestfallen," meaning disappointed, is the best choice to describe Sarah's emotion. The other choices do not make sense.
5	D	"Endangered," meaning in danger of becoming extinct, is the best choice. The other choices do not make sense in the sentence.
6	D	Although "said," "called," and "shrieked," are all verbs that could convey how a person spoke to another person, "whined" is the best fit in this sentence.
7	C	"Stammered," meaning stuttered, is the best word for the sentence.
8	D	"Hypothesis" is the best fit for the sentence. Scientists make hypotheses based on the evidence they have in order to explain an event.
9	C	"Critiqued," meaning evaluated or criticized, is the best fit for the sentence. "Agreed," does not make sense, and the other two choices are not fit to use in an academic context.
10	B	"Evidence" is the best choice for the sentence. The other words are related to reading but do not make sense in the sentence.

Notes

Frequently Asked Questions (FAQs)

SBAC FAQ

What will SBAC English Language Assessments Look Like?

In many ways, the SBAC assessments will be unlike anything many students have ever seen. The tests will be conducted online, requiring students complete tasks to assess a deeper understanding of the CCSS. The students will be assessed once 75% of the year has been completed in two different assessments - a Computer Adaptive Testing (CAT) and a Performance Task (PT).

The time for each ELA portion is described below:

Estimated Time on Task in Minutes		
Grade	CAT	PT
3	90	120
4	90	120
5	90	120
6	90	120
7	90	120
8	90	120

Bacause the assessment is online, the test will consist of a combination of new types of questions:

1. Drag and Drop
2. Drop Down
3. Essay Response
4. Extended Constructed Response
5. Hot Text Select and Drag
6. Hot Text Selective Highlight
7. Matching Table In-line
8. Matching Table Single Reponse
9. Multiple Choice – Single Correct Response, radial buttons
10. Multiple Choice – Multiple Response, checkboxes
11. Numeric Response
12. Short Text
13. Table Fill-in

What is this SBAC Test Practice Book?

Inside this book, you will find practice sections aligned to each CCSS. Students will have the ability to review questions on each standard, one section at a time, in the order presented, or they can choose to study the sections where they need the most practice.

In addition to the practice sections, you will have access to two full-length CAT and PT practice tests online. Completing these tests will help students master the different areas that are included in newly aligned SBAC tests and practice test taking skills. The results will help the students and educators get insights into students' strengths and weaknesses in specific content areas. These insights could be used to help students strengthen their skills in difficult topics and to improve speed and accuracy while taking the test.

Because the SBAC assessment includes newly created, technology-enhanced questions, it is necessary for students to be able to regularly practice these questions. The Lumos online StepUp program includes twelve technology enhanced questions that mimic the types students will see during the assessments. These include:

1. Drag and Drop

This style of question requires the student to move the correct answer from the answer choices into a box. Usually, this box is below the answer choices. If there is more than one box, click on the answer and drag it to the correct box. Hold the answer until it reaches the box and then release the mouse. Often, with multiple boxes, the student may need to continue holding and dragging down as the page scrolls to the correct box.

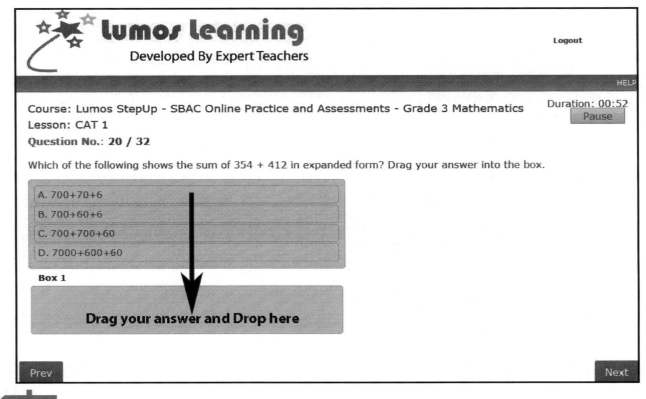

2. Drop Down

This style of question requires students to click on the drop down arrow and pull down the menu so they can select the correct answer.

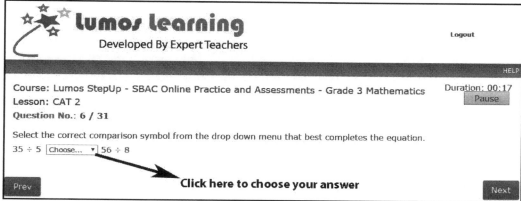

3. Essay Response

Essay response questions may be familiar to many students as they have been completing these types of responses for many years. The technology enhanced portion of this question though has the students typing their essay response into the box. As they type, the box will expand. Common word processing tools are available.

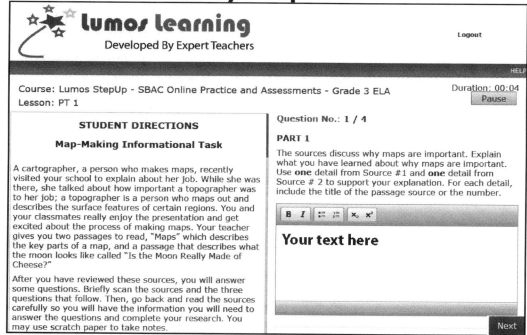

4.   Extended Constructed Response

Similar to Essay Response, the ECR allows students to write their responses to the question. These answers are not as long as essay responses but they are usually longer than just one or two words.

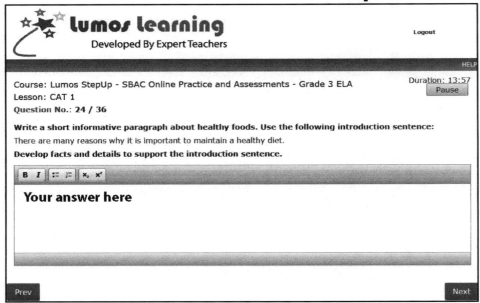

5.   Hot Text Select and Drag

With this style of questions, students must rearrange the text into the correct order. They might be asked to place events in a timeline, place an introductory sentence in the correct place, order information in the correct sequence, or any variety of tasks. Like a Drag and Drop, students can click on the highlighted sentence and move it where they would like it to be.

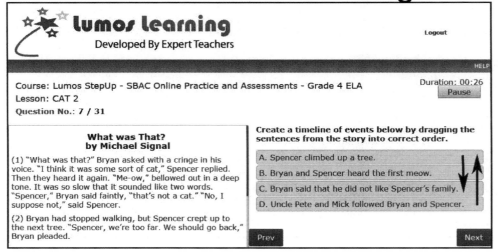

6.   Hot Text Selective Highlight

Hot Text – Selective Highlight asks students to select certain words or phrases from the paragraph for their answer. Often, this type of question will be used when students are asked for supporting information to defend an answer.

Hot Text - Selective Highlight

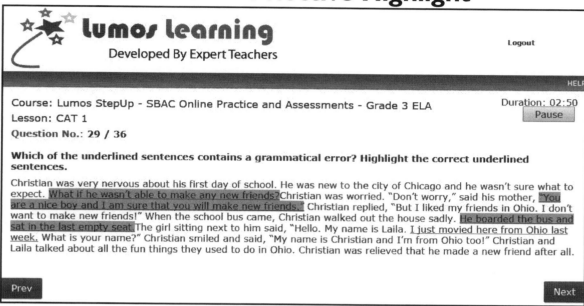

7.   Matching Table In-Line

This technology enhanced question requires students to process data spread across a table and mark check boxes. They may have one, or more than one, box selected in the table.

Matching Table - In-Line

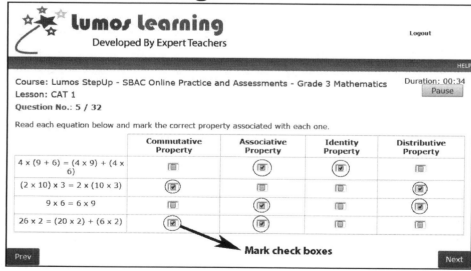

8.   Matching Table Single Response

Similar to the previous, Matching Table, students will make a selection in the table. With this type of question they will make a single choice such as yes/no or true/false.

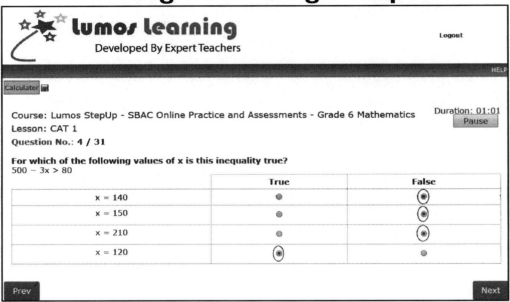

9.   Multiple Choice, Single Answer

This style of question is most similar to what students might recognize. It is a standard multiple choice with one answer.

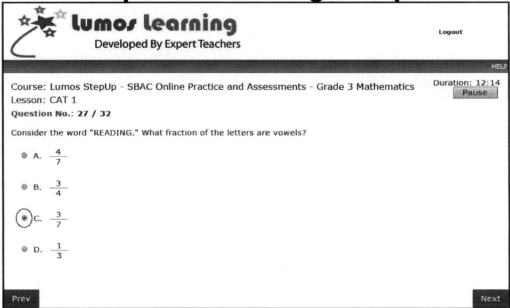

10.   Multiple Choice, Multiple Answer

Similar to the previous style, this question asks students to make a selection from options below. However, with the MCMA question, students will need to choose more than one answer. Careful reading of the question is required as it may offer guidance to the number of answer that need to be selected.

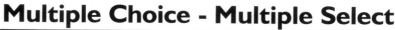

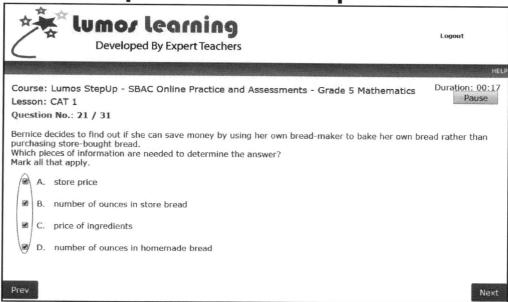

11.   Numeric Response

Numeric response questions have a small box where students can type in their solution to a problem. They might use numbers, words, or any combination of both. The question will typically offer guidance to what will go in the box.

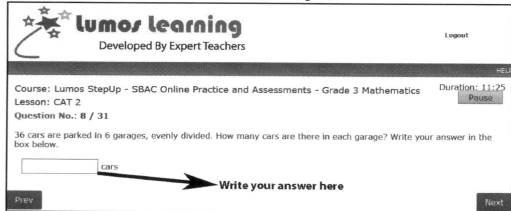

12. Short Constructed Response

Similar to an Extended Constructed Response, this question asks students to write short responses. Typically, students will use this box to explain how they arrive at a solution or why a response may be correct or incorrect.

Short Constructed Response

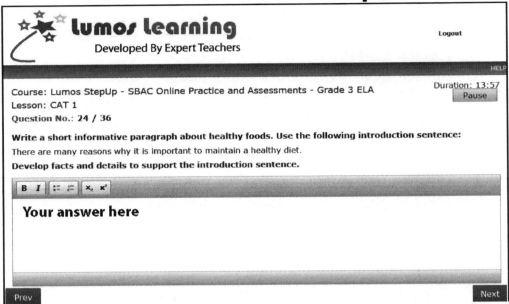

13. Table Fill In

This style of question requires students to fill in their answers.

Table Fill In

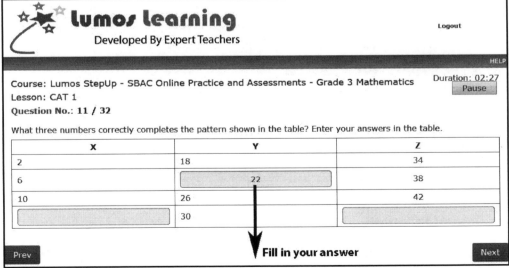

© Lumos Information Services 2015 | LumosLearning.com

How is this Lumos tedBook aligned to SBAC Guidelines?

The SBAC practice tests offered online at Lumos Learning have been created to accurately reflect the depth and rigor of SBAC. Students will still be exposed to the technology enhanced questions so they become familiar with the wording and how to think through these types of tasks.

This edition of the practice test book was created in the FALL 2015 and aligned to the most current SBAC standards released to date. Some changes will occur as SBAC continues to release new information in the spring of 2016 and beyond.

Lumos StepUp® Mobile App FAQ For Students

What is the Lumos StepUp® App?

It is a FREE application you can download onto your Android smart phones, tablets, iPhones, and iPads.

What are the Benefits of the StepUp® App?

This mobile application gives convenient access to Practice Tests, Common Core State Standards, Online Workbooks, and learning resources through your smart phone and tablet computers.
- Eleven Technology enhanced question types in both MATH and ELA
- Sample questions for Arithmetic drills
- Standard specific sample questions
- Instant access to the Common Core State Standards
- Jokes and cartoons to make learning fun!

Do I Need the StepUp® App to Access Online Workbooks?

No, you can access Lumos StepUp® Online Workbooks through a personal computer. The StepUp® app simply enhances your learning experience and allows you to conveniently access StepUp® Online Workbooks and additional resources through your smart phone or tablet.

How can I Download the App?

Visit **lumoslearning.com/a/stepup-app** using your smart phone or tablet and follow the instructions to download the app.

**QR Code
for Smart Phone
Or Tablet Users**

Lumos SchoolUp™ Mobile App FAQ
For Parents and Teachers

What is the Lumos SchoolUp™ App?

It is a FREE App that helps parents and teachers get a wide range of useful information about their school. It can be downloaded onto smartphones and tablets from popular App Stores.

What are the Benefits of the Lumos SchoolUp™ App?

It provides convenient access to

- School "Stickies". A Sticky could be information about an upcoming test, homework, extra curricular activities and other school events. Parents and educators can easily create their own sticky and share with the school community.
- Common Core State Standards.
- Educational blogs.
- StepUp™ student activity reports.

How can I Download the App?

Visit **lumoslearning.com/a/schoolup-app** using your smartphone or tablet and follow the instructions provided to download the App. Alternatively, scan the QR Code provided below using your smartphone or tablet computer.

QR Code
for Smart Phone
Or Tablet Users

The Lumos Learning Teacher Portal gives teachers insights into their students' work and access to useful resources. The personalized teacher dashboard includes six different tabs.

1. Student Reports

The 'Student Report' tab is the heart of the Teacher Portal. It is where teachers can create their student accounts, glean the most information about their list of students, class performance, individual student performance, and explore their list of subscribed content.

Progress Summary

This tab allows teachers to follow the progress of each of their students. From here, teachers can see overall progress of each student. They can then click on a specific student's name and see the individual details of progress. Additionally, teachers, can click on questions to be graded (essays and constructed responses for example).

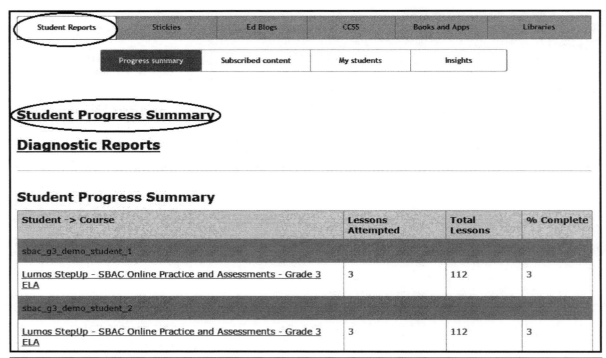

Subscribed Content

The subscribed content tab allows teachers to see all content to which they have subscribed. It is also from this tab that teachers can assign specific work to their students. A teacher can assign an individual lesson to the student through the 'View Worksheets' link; from there, the teacher can select from the list of lessons available. Students will then receive an alert about the assigned lesson.

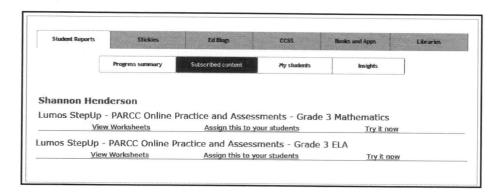

My Students

This tab allows teachers to see all login information for their assigned students. They can change passwords and create student accounts in this tab.

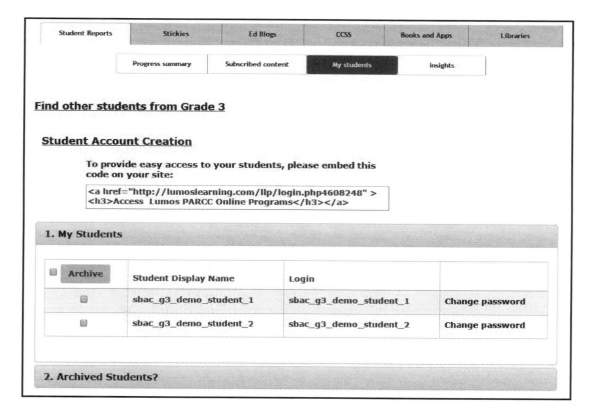

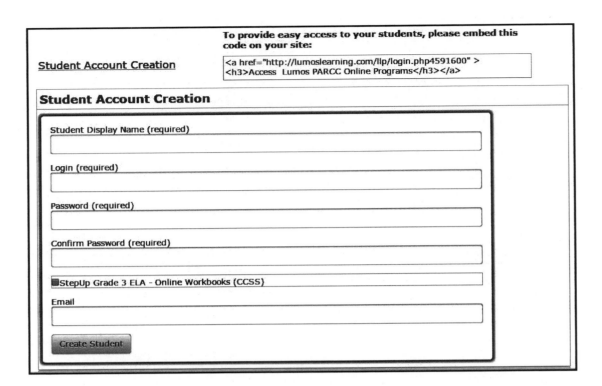

Insights

The insights tab is one of the most powerful parts of the teacher portal. It allows teachers to gain a deeper understanding of how their students are progressing. Individualized reports can be generated for specific date ranges. Student performance data can be categorized into partial, proficient, and advanced. Additionally, teachers can customize what guidelines they would like to stand for not meeting the standard (low bar), meeting the standard, and excelling above the standard. This report can be used to drive instruction and practice and identify what topics students might need additional assistance in to master the standard.

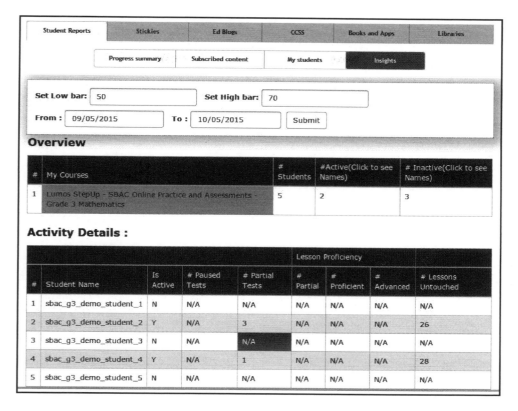

2. Stickies

Stickies are an exciting new way to share any type of school related information with parents and students.

- Need to share your school supply list?
- Have a great resource to exchange with others?
- Want to ensure parents can see a copy of the homework?
- Want to recommend a mobile app?
- Want to suggest a book?

Create a Stickie!

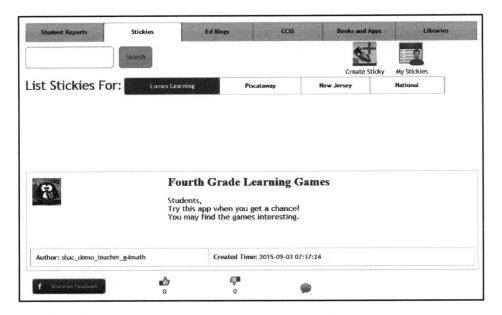

3. Ed Blogs

Lumos Learning teachers consistently monitor current educational trends and topics. Exploring the EdBlogs tab allows teachers to follow the blogs and stay current on important educational topics.

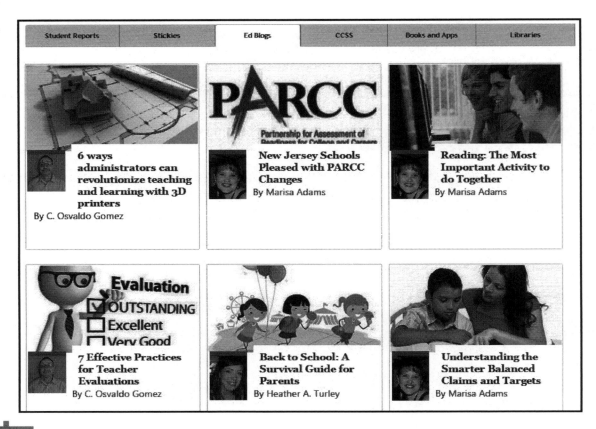

4. CCSS

With this tab, teachers are able to access the Common Core State Standards in one easy location. This eliminates the need to search in a variety of browsers to locate key information.

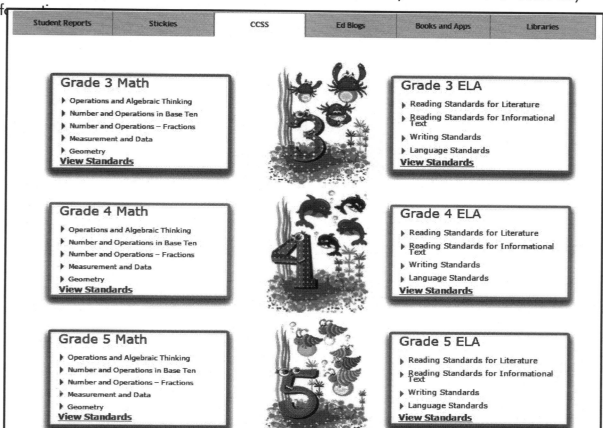

5. Books and Apps

This tab allows teachers to search for relevant educational books and apps. Teachers can easily recommend useful apps and books to their students by creating stickies.

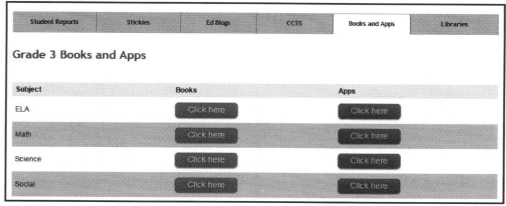

6. Libraries

Teachers can search their local libraries to look for educational books and other resources available in their area.

Student Reports	Stickies	Ed Blogs	CCSS	Books and Apps	Libraries

Libraries in Piscataway

Library Name	Address	Phone number
WESTERGARD LIBRARY	20 MURRAY AVE. PISCATAWAY Zip:8854	2017521166
PISCATAWAY PUBLIC LIBRARY	500 HOES LANE PISCATAWAY Zip:8854	2014631633

Lumos StepUp™ is an educational app that helps students learn and master grade-level skills in Math and English Language Arts.

The list of features includes:

- Learn Anywhere, Anytime!

- Grades 3-8 Mathematics and English Language Arts

- Get instant access to the Common Core State Standards

- One full-length sample practice test in all Grades and Subjects

- Full-length Practice Tests, Partial Tests and Standards-based Tests

- 2 Test Modes: Normal mode and Learning mode

- Learning Mode gives the user a step-by-step explanation if the answer is wrong

- Access to Online Workbooks

- Provides ability to directly scan QR Codes

- And it's completely FREE!

http://lumoslearning.com/a/stepup-app

Grade 4

SBAC Test Prep
Math

tedBook

Smarter Balanced Study Guide

ONLINE

2 Performance Tasks (PT)

2 Computer Adaptive Tests (CAT)

30+ SKILLS

Available

- At Leading book stores
- Online www.LumosLearning.com

MAR - - 2016

Made in the USA
Lexington, KY
13 March 2016